TRADITIONAL MUSICAL INSTRUMENTS
OF SOUTHERN ITALY

TRADITIONAL MUSICAL INSTRUMENTS OF SOUTHERN ITALY

ROSSELLA MARISI

COMMON GROUND

First published in 2025 as part of the
Arts in Society Book Imprint

Common Ground Research Networks
University of Illinois Research Park
2001 South First St, Suite 201L, Champaign, IL, 61820, USA

Library of Congress Cataloging-in-Publication Data

Names: Marisi, Rossella, author.
Title: Traditional music instruments of southern Italy / Rossella Marisi.
Description: Champaign, IL : Common Ground Research Networks, 2025. | Includes bibliographical references. | Summary: "In this book, readers are taken on an illuminating journey that identifies each traditional musical instrument from Southern Italy as part of the broader culture of the group of which the instrument is an expression. The study retraces the history of ethno-organology starting from its precursors and the accounts of early travelers. It draws connections between ethno-organology and other related sciences, such as ethnology, anthropology, musicology, organology, and ethnomusicology. Among the issues examined are the migration of musical instruments, various systems of musical instrument classification, and the analogies between pre-Christian era instruments and those still used today in traditional music. The instruments described are categorized as follows: idiophones include sistra, rattles, clappers, and ratchets; membranophones encompass cylindrical drums, frame drums, and friction drums; chordophones feature the colascione; and aerophones include bag aerophones, straight flutes, reed pipes, and the diatonic accordion. The book delves into each instrument's construction, usage contexts, performance nuances, evolutionary history, comparisons with similar instruments, and dissemination. It intertwines myths, rites, and historical events associated with the analyzed instruments to underscore their cultural significance, enriching understanding not just within their reference communities but for humanity at large" – Provided by publisher.
Identifiers: LCCN 2024059362 (print) | LCCN 2024059363 (ebook) | ISBN 9781966214182 (hardback) | ISBN 9781966214199 (paperback) | ISBN 9781966214205 (adobe pdf) Subjects: LCSH: Musical instruments – Italy, Southern – History. | Musical instruments, AncientvItaly, Southern – History. | Musical instruments – Social aspects – Italy, Southern – History. | Music archaeology – Italy, Southern. Classification: LCC ML503 .M37 2025 (print) | LCC ML503 (ebook) | DDC 784.0945/7 – dc23/eng/20141211

LC record available at https://lccn.loc.gov/2024059362
LC ebook record available at https://lccn.loc.gov/2024059363

Cover Image: Basilio Cascella, *Zampognaro*, n.d., oil on canvas, Private Collection of Mauro Gioielli, Italy
Cover Design: Phillip Kalantzis Cope

TABLE OF CONTENTS

INTRODUCTION

a) Musical Instruments as Part of Culture

The term "culture" has been interpreted in various ways throughout history. In ancient Greece, culture was regarded as a goal to be achieved over time through personal commitment, by studying philosophy, poetry, and rhetoric, and by engaging as spectators at the performance of tragedies. According to Plato, who lived between the 5th and the 4th centuries BCE and expressed his educational ideas in *The Republic* (Plato, 2009) and *The Laws* (Plato, 1934), and Aristotle, who lived in the 4th century BCE and addressed this subject in many of his works (Aristotle, 1984), all these forms of education enabled individuals to seek deeper truths by reflecting on themselves and the world around them. In ancient Rome, Cicero (who lived in the 1st century BCE) in the *Tusculanae Disputationes* [Tusculan Disputations] speaks of "cultura animi," referring to the function of culture in inner growth, which distinguishes an individual from the uncultured masses (Cicero, 1966: II, 13). In short, being cultured meant having a foundation of knowledge that fostered not only spiritual evolution but also the creation of new knowledge.

Over the centuries, the term "culture" acquired a broader meaning: in the Middle Ages, acquiring culture involved studying the liberal arts—grammar, rhetoric, dialectic, arithmetic, geometry, music, and astronomy. This notion of culture maintained an elitist character, privileging the contributions of recognized "geniuses" and assuming that only those with a broad and articulated education in these disciplines could be considered cultured and, therefore, bearers of culture. The obvious consequence was that illiterate populations and groups were not considered capable of developing their own cultural production.

However, toward the end of the 18th century, thanks to the reflections and proposals of some German intellectuals (Burke, 1978), the concept of popular culture (distinct from high culture) gradually emerged and became established. This concept encompassed the knowledge, beliefs, morals, customs, art, and law developed by society as a whole, including the popular strata (Tylor, 2010 [1871]).

During the Romantic period, the philosopher Johann Gottfried Herder (1744–1803), a scholar of popular traditions, advanced the innovative idea that the *Volksgeist*, or true spirit of the nation, is most fully expressed in oral poetry, songs, and popular dances (Herder, 2004). Thus, a new conception of culture emerged, one linked to the entire society that expressed it, rather than solely to individual formation and evolution.

This led to Bronislaw Malinowski's (1884–1942) formulation that culture is the set of knowledge and skills through which a society resolves its existential problems, interacting with the environment to meet its needs for food, shelter, defense, and so on (Malinowski, 1953). Malinowski emphasized that culture is a social heritage received from previous generations and passed on to future ones (Malinowski, 1944).

In the 1970s, there was a shift away from the "monumentalist" approach of the 1972 Convention for the Protection of the World Cultural and Natural Heritage, which focused on protecting monuments, buildings, and sites (Londres Fonseca, 2002), toward a new concept of cultural heritage that emphasized the protection of traditional and popular forms of culture.

In response to these demands, UNESCO launched the Intangible Cultural Heritage program in the early 1990s, aimed at preserving, revitalizing, and transmitting this form of cultural heritage. This led to the 2003 Convention for the Safeguarding of Intangible Cultural Heritage, which establishes:

Article 2—Definitions

For the purposes of this Convention:

1. The "intangible cultural heritage" means the practices, representations, expressions, knowledge, skills—as well as the instruments, objects, artifacts, and cultural spaces associated with them—that communities, groups, and, in some cases, individuals recognize as part of their cultural heritage. This intangible cultural heritage, transmitted from generation to generation, is constantly recreated by communities and groups in response to their environment, their interaction with nature, and their history, providing them with a sense of identity and continuity, thus promoting respect for cultural diversity and human creativity. For the purposes of this Convention, consideration will be given only to such intangible cultural heritage

that is compatible with existing international human rights instruments, as well as with the requirements of mutual respect among communities, groups, and individuals, and of sustainable development.

2.   The "intangible cultural heritage," as defined in paragraph 1 above, is manifested in the following domains: (a) oral traditions and expressions, including language as a vehicle of intangible cultural heritage; (b) performing arts; (c) social practices, rituals, and festive events; (d) knowledge and practices concerning nature and the universe; (e) traditional craftsmanship (...). (UNESCO, 2003)

According to these definitions, as established by the Convention, "instruments, objects, artifacts [definitions that can also be applied to musical instruments] and cultural spaces associated with them" are part of the intangible cultural heritage, manifesting in "traditions," "performing arts, social practices, rituals, and festive events," and "traditional craftsmanship." These must be safeguarded, ensuring respect for them and raising awareness of their importance, as prescribed by Article 1 of the same Convention.

Therefore, traditional musical instruments, the way they are played, and the social and ritual occasions in which they are used are of central importance, not only for the society and culture that expressed them but also for humanity as a whole.

b) Globalization and Identity Crisis

Globalization, the development of strong economic, political, and cultural interconnections on a global scale (McGrew, 2008), can be seen as a positive phenomenon that allows for the broad and rapid sharing of knowledge, as well as of scientific and technological innovations, access to goods previously unavailable in specific areas, and the spread of awareness of the benefits of international collaboration. All these aspects seem to lead toward an orientation defined by some scholars as "cosmopolitan," which views favorably the access to new cultures and new ways of thinking and acting (Norris, 2000). However, the other side of globalization presents less positive aspects, stemming from the fact that the merging of different cultures often results in the success of some cultures at the expense of others; the latter then tend to lose their distinctive characteristics, leading to a loss of cultural richness on a global level, and to appear less attractive to their own adherents, who may experience a crisis of identity and traditional values. There is even the risk of homogenization of culture and, similarly, of musical practices (Guilbault, 2007).

In short, a phenomenon like the one that has seen the national language gain ground over the use of dialects may occur. The national language's greater use, not limited to domestic and familial contexts, its greater prestige, and its ability to denote new ideas and objects with appropriate terms that did not previously exist, have led to the gradual abandonment of dialects. This has resulted not only in a reduction of the dialect's lexical richness but also in the younger generations' inability to understand aspects of their grandparents' and great-grandparents' lifestyles (traditions, objects, tools, trades, techniques used in agriculture), leading to a loss of cultural roots and of a sense of belonging (Gramellini, 2008).

The spread of classical music, like other currently popular musical genres, could correspond to a crisis in traditional music, whose practice and enjoyment might become increasingly marginalized.

c) Oral Traditional Music and Written Music: Two Separate Worlds?

A similar scenario to that of the relationship between the use of national language and dialect could be envisaged for traditional music, which is passed down orally, in contrast to classical music, which has been transmitted in written form for many centuries. As Walter Ong suggests for poetic works, while orally trans-mitted poems and songs result from an interaction between the performer, the performer's memories of past performances, and the current audience, with the originality of a performer lying in how they relate to the latter, written poems and musical pieces tend to be seen as definitive objects (Ong, 2002). Molino also distinguishes between written music and music of oral tradition, identifying the main difference in the role of the performer: in written music, the variability of a single performance concerns only the interpretative aspect, whereas in oral traditional music, the performer varies the piece on multiple levels, from basic units to motifs and sequences (Molino, 2007).

According to this perspective, one might imagine that written music and the "petrification" of traditional music when recorded and then transcribed represent an entirely different and distant realm from true oral traditional music, preventing any fruitful interchange between the two.

On the contrary, history has shown that the attention of various classical music composers to the melodic-rhythmic patterns and timbres of traditional music can lead to very fruitful interactions. Examples can be found in several works by Claude Debussy: for instance, in *Iberia*, where the composer incorporates melodic-rhythmic patterns from the Spanish folk tradition; in *Pagodes*, where he recreates the sounds of the Javanese gamelan on the piano; and in *La sérénade interrompue*, where explicit instructions in the score prescribe a touch that makes the piano resemble the sound of a flamenco guitar. Other examples include the "recreation" of performing practices and timbres of traditional and folk music instruments using classical instruments. Examples of this include Ferenc Liszt's imitation of the gypsy violin bow stroke and the timbre of the Hungarian cimbalom on the piano in the second and third of his *Hungarian Rhapsodies*, as well as Igor Stravinskij's evocation of the sound of the ancient Slavic folk bagpipe, the *dudki*, on the bassoon in *The Rite of Spring*. Finally, an even more intriguing aspect is the combination of timbres from traditional and folk instruments with those of classical instruments, as achieved by Piero Niro in his composition *Note per il Molise* [Notes for Molise], for zampogna, *ciaramella*, and strings.

Therefore, it can be concluded that there can be a fruitful exchange between traditional and folk music, on the one hand, and classical music, on the other, and that enthusiasts and scholars of classical music can find, within the realm of traditional music, food for thought that allows them to identify analogies and derivations between the two domains. This understanding can lead to a more comprehensive appreciation of the ideal references drawn from traditional music that have guided specific choices made by classical music composers regarding forms, melodic motifs, rhythmic cells, and timbral suggestions.

d) Guiding Principles and Structure of this Volume

The main idea of this volume is to contribute to the knowledge of traditional instruments of southern Italy, not only by describing them but also by illustrating playing techniques, combinations with other instruments, and especially the occasions for use and their connections with dance, singing, and various civil and religious ceremonies. The aim is to guide readers to understand not only the simple construction aspects of each instrument but also the broader cultural aspects surrounding it.

For the same reasons, where known, the dialectal names of the instruments and their parts are provided, along with their specific etymologies: all these elements can contribute to the cultural placement of the instruments and their use.

The focus is on traditional musical instruments found in southern Italy (Fig. 1), with the conviction that the centuries-old common history of these areas has given rise to instruments characterized by shared peculiarities, as well as inevitable differences due to various local traditions. To promote the contextualization of the knowledge gradually acquired, references are provided to similar instruments found in other areas of Italy and other countries.

Fig. 1 Map of Southern Italy 1: Latium 2: Abruzzo 3: Molise 4: Campania 5: Apulia 6: Basilicata 7: Calabria 8: Sicily 9: Sardinia

This volume is divided into three parts: the first, titled *What Is Ethno-Organology?* includes Chapters 1–7; the second, titled *Analogies Between Archaeological Finds and Modern Instruments*, includes Chapters 8 and 9; and the third, titled *Occasions and Instruments of Oral Traditional Music*, includes Chapters 10–15.

More specifically, in Part 1, Chapter 1 defines the field of research; Chapter 2 reflects on the concept of a musical instrument; Chapter 3 clarifies which characteristics of the instruments are studied in ethno-organology; Chapter 4 focuses on scholars active between the late 15th century and the early 20th century who can be considered precursors of ethno-organology; Chapter 5 focuses on what the accounts of great travelers who traveled through Italy between the 18th and the 19th centuries report about traditional music and the instruments of southern Italy; Chapter 6 discusses the effects on musical instruments when they migrate from one territory to another; and Chapter 7 illustrates the main classifications of musical instruments proposed over time in both European and non-European contexts.

In Part 2, Chapter 8 examines some instruments from before the Common Era found in different areas of southern Italy and present in various museums; and Chapter 9 analyzes various instruments like those described in Chapter 8, still in use in the same areas.

In Part 3, Chapter 10 considers various occasions on which oral traditional music is performed, including work songs, devotional songs, and historical reenactments. Chapters 11–14 each focus on one of the classes of instruments used in traditional music. The discussion of many instruments already analyzed in Part 2, Chapter 9, is not repeated in this part. Chapter 11 examines idiophones found in Abruzzo, Apulia, Sicily, and Sardinia; Chapter 12 deals with membranophones present in Abruzzo, Molise, Sicily, and Sardinia; Chapter 13, centered on chordophones, presents the colascione, used today in both traditional and ancient music; and Chapter 14 focuses on various types of aerophones, including free aerophones, free reed aerophones, recorder flutes, bagpipes, and reedpipes. Finally, Chapter 15 presents a synoptic table of the various instruments analyzed.

Further Reading and Online Resources

Aristotle. *The Complete Works of Aristotle: The Revised Oxford Translation*, edited by Jonathan Barnes. Princeton, NJ: Princeton University Press, 1984.

Burke, Peter. *Popular Culture in Early Modern Europe*. New York: Harper-Collins College Div., 1978.

Cicero. *Tusculan Disputations*, translated by J. E. King. Cambridge, MA: Harvard University Press—London: William Heinemann, 1966.

Gramellini, Flavia. "Il dialetto del nuovo millennio: usi, parlanti, apprendenti." *Ianua. Rivista Philologica Romanica*, 8, 2008: 181–201.

Guilbault, Jocelyne. "Mondialisation et localisme." In *Musiques*. Une Ency-clopédie pour le XXIe siècle, edited by Jean-Jacques Nattiez, V, *L'unité de la musique*, 313–334. Arles-Paris: Actes Sud/Cité de la musique, 2007."

Herder, Johann Gottfried. *Another Philosophy of History and Selected Political Writings*, translated by Ioannis D. Evrigenis and Daniel Pellerin. Indianapolis, IN: Hackett Publishing, 2004.

Londres Fonseca, Maria Cecilia. "Intangible Cultural Heritage and Museum Exhibitions." *ICOM UK News*, 63, 2002: 8–9.

Malinowski, Bronislaw. *A Scientific Theory of Culture and Other Essays*. Chapel Hill: University of North Carolina Press, 1944.

Malinowski, Bronislaw. *Essays on Culture*. Madison: University of Wisconsin Press, 1953.

McGrew, Anthony. "Globalization and Global Politics." In *The Globalization of World Politics: An Introduction to International Relations*, edited by John Baylis, Steve Smith, and Patricia Owens, 14–31. Oxford: Oxford University Press, 2008.

Molino, Jean. "Qu'est-ce que l'oralité musicale?" In *Musiques. Une encyclopédie pour le XXIe siècle*, edited by Jean-Jacques Nattiez, V, *L'unité de la musique*, 477–527. Arles-Paris: Actes Sud/Cité de la musique, 2007."

Norris, Pippa. "Global Governance and Cosmopolitan Citizens." In *Gover-nance in a Globalizing World*, edited by Joseph D. Nye and John D. Donahue, 155–177. Washington, DC: Brooking Institution Press, 2000.

Ong, Walter J. *Orality and Literacy: The Technologizing of the Word*. New York: Routledge, 2002.

Plato. *The Laws*, translated by A. E. Taylor. London: Dent & Sons, 1934.

Plato. "The Republic," translated by Benjamin Jowett, 2009. Accessed November 3, 2024. https://classics.mit.edu/Plato/republic.html.

Tylor, Edward Burnett. *Primitive Culture*. Cambridge: Cambridge University Press, 2010 (1871).

UNESCO. "Text of the Convention for the Safeguarding of the Intangible Cultural Heritage," 2003. Accessed November 3, 2024. https://ich.unesco.org /en/convention.

PART 1

What Is Ethno-Organology?

CHAPTER 1

Ethno-Organology: Definition of the Research Field

To introduce the concept of ethno-organology, it is essential to first consider its name, which offers several clues about its scope. The term "ethno-organology" is a compound word comprising three elements: ethno-, -organo-, and -logy. Starting from the end, -logy derives from the Greek *logos*, which has various meanings, including reflection, word, discourse, and logical structuring. Thus, a compound ending in -logy signifies the discourse, reflection, or study around a specific theme, as indicated in the first part of the compound. In this case, ethno-organo-logy refers to the discourse and reflection on topics related to the subjects indicated by the first word elements.

The central element of the compound, -organo-, is derived from the Greek *organon*, which refers in a general way to musical instruments. Thus, it encompasses not only organs but all types of musical instruments. The similarity between the term *organ*, referring to the instrument commonly played in churches, and organo-, used in compound words like organology and organological, can lead to linguistic inaccuracies or misunderstandings. Consequently, some scholars choose to call this field of investigation the "history and technology of musical instruments" to avoid confusion (Meucci, 2006).

Regardless of whether the field is termed "history and technology of musical instruments" or "organology," it consistently investigates musical instruments, examining the circular relationships among:

- Construction techniques,
- Performance practices, and
- Musical aesthetics, within their historical-cultural contexts.

Next, we need to define the word element ethno-, which also comes from Greek, specifically from the noun *ethnos*, meaning people of the same nation, group, tribe, or race.

Let's delve further into the name of the discipline, ethno-organology. By combining the first word element, ethno-, with the third one, -logy, we get the term ethnology, coined in 1783 by scholar Adam František Kollár (1718–1783). According to Kollár, ethnology is "the science of nations and peoples, or the study of learned men in which they inquire into the origins, languages, customs, and institutions of various nations" (Kollár, 1783: I, 80). Ethnology specifically explores themes related to a group of people belonging to the same nation, tribe, or ethnicity, and therefore sharing a common culture and language.

Now we can integrate the meanings from the three word elements of the compound ethno-organology. This field of science examines the musical instruments of a specific group or nation, particularly focusing on issues related to construction techniques, performance practices, and musical aesthetics within their historical-cultural contexts. According to scholar Thor Magnusson, ethno-organology encompasses not only the descriptive analysis of musical instruments but also the technological evolution of instruments related to the social history of the ethnic group that created and used them, as well as various methods of instrument classification (Magnusson, 2021).

It is important to highlight that ethno-organology is a discipline contributing to the broader field of ethnomusicology. As inferred from the foregoing discussion, ethnomusicology:

• Like musicology, studies sounds organized by humans to form music.
• Like anthropology, explores how and why humans express their musicality.

However, defining musicology simply as "the study of sounds organized by humans to form music" can be somewhat limiting. Firstly, it is important to remember that in other cultures (or even in the West during past historical periods, such as in ancient Greece), the term music encompasses singing, instrumental performance, dance, clapping, and more. Secondly, music is generally understood as a product rather than a process. For example, in early ethnomusicological studies, researchers focused on specific elements and structures of music, captured through recordings or even musical notation (Nelson, 2012). However, this approach of "fixing" the performance overlooked many important aspects, such as the interactions between performers, between the audience, and between performers and the audience, and the meanings behind these behaviors.

For these reasons, contemporary scholars prefer to understand musicology as the study of people making music, exploring how and why they make music

(Rice, 2014). This perspective equally applies to ethnomusicology, which can be broadly defined as the study of an ethnic group making music and the cultural significance of these practices.

Ethnomusicology shares elements with musicology and anthropology but diverges from these disciplines in some fundamental respects. Specifically, ethnomusicology:

- Studies how certain ethnic groups make music.
- Focuses predominantly on traditional music, which differs from classical music.

Summing up, ethno-organology is the study and reflection on the musical instruments of traditional music, which for a long time were used exclusively to produce music from an oral tradition.

What is meant by the term *oral traditional music*?

Oral traditional music refers to music whose modes of transmission prioritize performance—the act of making music—over written parts, treatises, and academic teaching. Here, we revisit the concept of ethnomusicology as the study of how certain groups create music.

In the phrase *oral tradition*, the last term is *tradition*. This refers to a specific context in which all those involved, both performers and listeners, explicitly refer to the idea of *tradition*, meaning the continuity of knowledge transmission from generation to generation, as mentioned earlier, through oral means.

Finally, it is appropriate to reflect on what a *musical instrument* is. Fundamentally, a musical instrument is an object that produces sound or sounds. Such an object may not even be originally intended for musical purposes: for instance, the anvil, a tool used by blacksmiths, was used as a musical instrument by Gustav Mahler (1860-1911) in his *Fourth Symphony*.

So what turns an object that produces sound into a true musical instrument? The key factor is its conscious use in performative and ritual contexts.

Summary

The first part of this book, titled *What Is Ethno-Organology?* consists of Chapters 1–7. Chapter 1 introduces readers to the world of ethno-organology, guiding them step by step from foundational definitions to situating the discipline within a broader context of related fields. The term ethno-organology is defined, clarifying the scope and focus of this field. The chapter explores the relationships and distinctions between ethno-organology and other disciplines such as ethnology, which investigates the origins, languages, customs, and institutions of various nations; musicology, which is the study of sounds organized by humans to create music; and anthropology, which studies, among other topics, how and why humans express their musicality. The scope of ethno-organology encompasses not only the descriptive analysis of musical instruments but also their technological evolution related to the social history of the ethnic groups that created and used them. Additionally, it examines various methods for classifying instruments. This chapter also delves into the meaning of *oral traditional music*, referring to music passed down orally from generation to generation and offers a preliminary explanation of what is meant by the term *musical instrument*.

Keywords

Anthropology, Construction Techniques, Ethno-Organology, Ethnology, History and Technology of Musical Instruments, Musical Aesthetics, Musical Instrument, Musicology, Oral Traditional Music, Performance Practices, Tradition.

Preeminent Figures

Adam František Kollár
Thor Magnusson

Questions for Review

1. What is the definition and scope of ethno-organology?
2. On which fields of knowledge does ethno-organology focus its research?
3. Should music be seen more as a product or as a process?
4. What similarities and differences can be found among ethnomusicology, musicology, and anthropology?
5. What does the term *oral traditional music* refer to?
6. Under what conditions can an object that produces sounds be called a musical instrument?

Further Readings and Online Resources

Kollár, Adam František. *Historiae jurisqve pvblici regni Ungariae amoenitates.* Vienna: Typis A. Baumeisterianis, 1783.

Magnusson, Thor. "The Migration of Musical Instruments: On the Socio-Technological Conditions of Musical Evolution." *Journal of New Music Research*, 50(2), 2021: 175–183.

Meucci, Renato. "Fondamenti di organologia musicale." In *Alla ricerca dei suoni perduti. Arte e musica negli strumenti della collezione di Fernanda Giulini*, edited by John Henry van der Meer, 598–617. Milano, Italy: Villa Medici Giulini, 2006.

Nelson, David Taylor. "The Father of Ethnomusicology." *Musical Offerings*, 3(2), 2012: 75–91.

Rice, Timothy. *Ethnomusicology: A Very Short Introduction*. Oxford/New York: Oxford University Press, 2014.

CHAPTER 2

What Is a Musical Instrument?

Musicologist Febo Guizzi, in his *Guida alla musica popolare in Italia* [Guide to Italian Popular Music], begins his exploration by suggesting that human communication inherently relies on sound messages. Over time, this reliance leads to the adoption of objects specifically designed for producing and transmitting these communication messages (Guizzi, 2020). Musical instruments represent a prominent category of such objects.

Access to musical instruments is influenced by several factors:

- **Social Group Affiliation:** Access varies among different social groups, such as farmers, sailors, artisans, and itinerant workers.
- **Wealth and Social Status:** The affordability of instruments and the level of education required to play them are influenced by one's economic standing and social class.
- **Physical Aptitude:** Playing certain instruments, like the piano or the organ, necessitates specific physical attributes for proficiency, such as hand size.
- **Exposure:** Familiarity with an instrument's sound is crucial; exposure shapes one's affinity toward specific instruments.
- **Influence of Authoritative Figures:** Guidance from influential individuals can either encourage or discourage the pursuit of playing certain instruments.
- **Personal Preference:** Individual taste plays a pivotal role in instrument selection, driving preferences and rejections based on subjective affinity.

These variables collectively determine an individual's access to and relationship with musical instruments, reflecting broader social dynamics and personal inclinations in musical engagement. The combination of these variables determines:

1. Whether one has access to one or more musical instruments.
2. Whether one possesses them for use on different occasions.
3. Whether one can benefit from manuals and lessons provided by experts who can facilitate the learning process.

Another significant factor influencing the dissemination of instruments is the route by which they enter the market. Traditional and popular musical instruments are often sold at venues such as fairs, religious festivals, and locations near popular worship sites. These places host bustling markets where sellers interact with pilgrim-buyers.

When instruments are bought/sold outside conventional musical circuits, there is typically little attention given to their musical properties, such as tuning accuracy or timbre quality. Sellers often lack expertise in musical matters, while buyers may be novices or amateurs with limited experience with the instrument. Instruments sold in these "market stall" settings are often chosen based on nonmusical attributes:

1. **Affordability:** Especially if musical instruments are intended as gifts for children and teenagers, their affordability is key, given the uncertainty of whether the recipients will continue playing long enough to justify a significant financial investment.
2. **Aesthetic Appeal:** Instruments may be chosen for their decorations or colorful ribbons and are often used more as home decor than as musical instruments to be played systematically. These instruments might be visually striking and are frequently displayed as souvenirs of trips or events.

The dissemination of instruments beyond their original context involves various circumstances:

1. **Performers' Travels:** Performers were driven by musical tours or employment reasons like transhumance, commercial ventures, and military campaigns.
2. **Acquisition by Enthusiasts and Scholars:** Instruments are sometimes purchased by enthusiasts and scholars from other cultures. For example, Johann Wilde, a German musician at the St. Petersburg court around 1750, acquired and learned to play a sheng, an ancient instrument considered a precursor to free reed instruments (Sachs, 1913). Another example is Filippo Bonanni, who in 1722 published *Gabinetto armonico pieno d'istromenti sonori, indicati e spiegati* [Musical Cabinet Full of Sounding Instruments, Shown and Explained] describing and illustrating instruments

from museum housed within the Collegio Romano dei Gesuiti in Rome, where he served as curator after Athanasius Kircher. This treatise included instruments like the piva and the musette (Bonanni, 1722).

3. **Migration:** The migration of members from the original ethnic group to new areas often leads to the gradual adoption of their instruments. For example, Sicily has experienced various dominations throughout history, such as Greek colonization from the 8th to the 3rd century BCE and Islamic rule from 827 to 1091 CE, involving peoples native to, or originating from, Africa. These periods contributed to the introduction and spread of both Greek and African-origin instruments in Sicily.

Considering historical migrations, commercial ventures, and military expeditions from centuries ago:

1. These movements likely impacted numerous nearby regions over time, making it challenging, if not impossible, to precisely trace the paths taken by instruments and the timing of their introduction.
2. Instruments preserved from these times often exhibit characteristics indicative of their original imports, as well as influences from local construction techniques and musical practices. This cultural exchange illustrates the dynamic nature of culture, which evolves rather than remains static.

However, the possibility of "contaminations" should also be considered with regard to revival operations. When considering revival efforts—such as attempts to revive dances, musical forms, or the use of obsolete instruments—Febo Guizzi cautions against approaching these initiatives with a contemporary mindset. In his view, revival initiatives are often guided by modern perspectives rather than those characterizing the historical eras they seek to revive (Guizzi, 2020).

Summary

Human communication is inseparable from the use of sound messages, leading to the development of objects specifically designed to produce and transmit these messages over time. Among these objects are musical instruments. Access to musical instruments depends on several factors: social group affiliation, belonging to a certain economic and social class, physical ability, exposure to specific instruments, influence from authoritative figures, and personal preferences. The combination of these factors determines whether individuals have access to musical instruments, possess them for various occasions, and can benefit from manuals and lessons provided by skilled instructors to facilitate their learning.

Another factor influencing the diffusion of musical instruments is their distribution channels. Traditional and popular instruments are often sold at fairs and during religious festivals. The spread of an instrument beyond its place of origin is influenced by various circumstances such as travels of performers, interest and acquisition by scholars from other cultures, and migration of members of the original ethnic group to new regions.

Keywords

Aesthetic Appeal, Affordability, Commercial Ventures, Dissemination of Instruments Beyond Their Original Context, Exposure, Fairs, Historical Migrations, Influence of Authoritative Figures, Military Expeditions, Nonmusical Attributes, Personal Preference, Physical Aptitude, Revival Initiatives, Social Group Affiliation, Social Status, Timbre Quality, Tuning Accuracy.

Preeminent Figures

- Febo Guizzi
- Johann Wilde
- Filippo Bonanni

Questions for Review

1. In what sense can it be said that musical instruments produce and transmit messages of communication?
2. What variables affect access to specific musical instruments and the appropriate educational pathways related to their use?
3. In what ways can a musical instrument reach the market?
4. Are there extra-musical reasons that might encourage the purchase of a musical instrument?

5. What circumstances can influence the spread of an instrument beyond the area of its "invention"?
6. Is it always possible to precisely identify the path taken by an instrument from the area of its "invention" to the regions where it has spread?
7. What characteristics of an instrument might indicate its "importation" or its "contamination"?
8. Is there a possibility of "contamination" in the revival efforts?

Further Reading and Online Resources

Bonanni, Filippo. *Gabinetto armonico pieno d'istromenti sonori, indicati e spiegati dal padre Filippo Bonanni della Compagnia di Gesù offerto al Santo Re David.* Roma: Giorgio Placho, 1722.

Guizzi, Febo. *Guida alla musica popolare in Italia.* Lucca, Italy: LIM, 2020.

Sachs, Curt. *Real-Lexikon der Musikinstrumente zugleich ein Polyglossar für das gesamte Instrumentengebiet.* Berlin: Julius Bard, 1913.

CHAPTER 3

Characteristics of Musical Instruments Studied in Ethno-Organology

In ethno-organology, the study of musical instruments encompasses several characteristics, including the following:

- **Name of the Instrument and Its Parts:** Often, these names are onomatopoeic in origin. For instance, the instrument called *triccheballacche* derives its name from the dry sound it produces. In other cases, the name refers to the effect of the instrument's sound, such as *scetavajasse*, meaning "waking up servants." Sometimes, the name relates to the materials used in its construction, like *ciaramella*, possibly derived from the Latin *calamus*, meaning reed.
- **Instrument's History and Geographical Dissemination:** The history of an instrument, including where it is found, can be gleaned not only from surviving specimens but also from iconography and written records. However, this information must be carefully examined as memory and artistic interpretation may have altered some details.
- **Shape and Construction:** This includes the general design, the various parts, the materials used, and the best practices for sourcing these materials—through both plant cultivation and animal husbandry. It also covers the timing and techniques for obtaining the raw materials needed to achieve the desired sound, as well as the methods and the processes for crafting the instrument.
- **Performance Technique and Repertoire:** *Performance technique* refers to a set of specialized gestures that, after exploring the instrument's musical potential, actualize the most interesting and creative possibilities. The repertoire depends on the instrument's structure and range, the performer's skill, their learning possibilities and the methods of learning used. Whether the instrument is used solo or in accompaniment affects

the repertoire, as do the types of other instruments with which it is played, the occasions for performance and listening, as well as opportunities for exchanging experience.

- **Physical Context of Use:** The shape and size of an instrument influence how it is played and the performer's movements, which in turn dictate the space needed for the performance. For example, the telharmonium, invented by Thaddeus Cahill around 1897, was very massive and bulky: it weighed about 200 tons and was so large it could not be transported or played outside a specific venue.

- **Social Context of Use:** Some instruments are tied to specific rituals, such as festive or funeral bell tolls, Christmas chants, or Easter traditions. These rituals often involve most inhabitants of a community, giving the music strong social significance. Instruments and the music produced with them also play roles in military, hunting, or work contexts.

- **Social Status of the Performer:** The social status of those who play certain instruments can vary depending on the social context in which an instrument is played. For instance, in 1500s England, lute players held a higher social status, as lute was considered an instrument of "high music," often played in the presence of royalty. According to sociologist Max Weber, lute players in Queen Elizabeth I's court were paid five times more than bagpipe players due to the instrument's "intrinsic nobility" (Weber, 1958).

- **Function of the Performance:** Among the most common functions of a musical performance are the following: ritual function, when the performance is carried out to accompany religious ceremonies; ceremonial function, when the performance is carried out to accompany civil ceremonies, which happens, for example, when national anthems are played during the awarding of athletes at international sporting events; hedonistic function, that is, aimed at the pleasure of listening, as occurs, for example, in concerts; pedagogical function, when the teacher performs a piece in front of their student to demonstrate technical and stylistic aspects of the performance; therapeutic function, which was traditionally realized when specific sounds and musical sequences were performed by shamans, and today in sessions of sound therapy and music therapy; function of accompaniment to dance; command and accompaniment function for military maneuvers, and so on.

- **Relationship Between Instruments Used Together:** An example of this is the 1600s combination of trumpets and timpani, where the timpani supported the sound of the trumpets, achieving a compact and balanced sound.
- **Relationship Between Instrument and Performer:** Some instruments are reserved for specific classes or professions, such as the sistra in ancient Egypt, which were played only by priests. Additionally, this occurs whenever a particular instrumental sound is given a "meaning" derived from the gestures the performer uses to produce the sounds. Examples include the "harsher" sounds produced by striking certain percussion instruments with dedicated mallets and, conversely, the "softer" sounds of gentle glissandos on the harp, for which the harpist's fingers almost "caress" the strings of the instrument.
- **Relationship Between Instrument and Listeners:** This includes the cultural and aesthetic implications of using a particular instrument in a specific context.

All these elements contribute to the overall "meaning" of using a particular musical instrument in a given circumstance.

For these reasons, the study of ethno-organology is not limited to simply describing instruments but is connected to:

- **Musicology:** The broader "science of music."
- **Organology:** The study and reflection on musical instruments in general.
- **Anthropology:** The study of human beings, combining sociological, cultural, artistic, and philosophical-religious perspectives.
- **Ethnology:** The investigation of themes related to a group of people belonging to the same nation, tribe, or ethnicity, sharing the same culture and language.
- **Ethnomusicology:** The discipline that includes ethno-organology as an integral part.

Ethno-organology examines each instrument as a node in a conceptual network connected to several other nodes, sharing aspects, methods of investigation, and perspectives. This network, in turn, constitutes the broader culture of the group or people whom the instrument represents.

Having outlined the research field of ethno-organology, we can ask whether it is a recent discipline or whether certain ideas anticipating ethno-organological perspectives can be identified in works published over the course of centuries.

Ethno-organology is part of ethnomusicology, a discipline that emerged from comparative musicology, which developed between the late 19th and the early 20th centuries. As its name suggests, comparative musicology studied musical products from different cultures, believing that such studies could shed light on fundamental issues related to human evolution. After World War II, a new field of study emerged in the US, which Jaap Kunst named "ethnomusicology" (Kunst, 1950). Scholarly works in this discipline, such as those by Willard Rhodes (1956), Alan Merriam (1964), Alan Lomax (2005), and Timothy Rice (2014), were inspired by methods used in cultural anthropology, shifting away from comparative analyses of different cultures' products and instead focusing on in-depth studies of individual cultures.

Summary

Among the characteristics of musical instruments studied in ethno-organology are: 1) the name of the instrument and its parts; 2) the history of the instrument and its geographical dissemination; 3) the instrument's shape, construction design, components, and materials used; 4) the playing technique and repertoire; 5) the physical context of its use, including the spatial and temporal characteristics of its setting; 6) the social context of its use; 7) the social status of the performers; 8) the function of the performance; 9) the relationship between the instrument and other instruments used in the same performance; 10) the relationship between instrument and performer; 11) the cultural and aesthetic implications of its use.

Keywords

Comparative Musicology, Function of the Performance, Geographical Distribution, History of the Instrument, Iconography, Name of the Instrument, Performance Technique, Physical Context, Relationship Between Instrument and Listeners, Relationship Between Instrument and Performer, Relationship Between the Instruments Used in the Same Performance, Repertoire, Shape of the Instrument, Social Context, Social Status of the Performer, Written Records.

Preeminent Figures

- Alan Lomax
- Alan Merriam
- Jaap Kunst
- Max Weber
- Thaddeus Cahill
- Timothy Rice
- William Rhodes

Questions for Review

1. What insights can the name of an instrument provide?
2. What sources can be used to gather information about the history and the geographical spread of an instrument?
3. What factors should be considered regarding the materials used in the construction of an instrument?
4. What is meant by playing technique and repertoire?
5. What do the physical and social context in which an instrument is used refer to?
6. What factors can influence the social status of the performer?
7. What functions can a musical performance fulfill?
8. When did the shift from comparative musicology to ethnomusicology occur?

Further Reading and Online Resources

Kunst, Jaap. *Musicologica: A Study of the Nature of Ethno-Musicology, Its Problems, Methods and Representative Personalities*. Amsterdam: Indisch Institut, 1950.

Lomax, Alan. *Selected Writings 1934–1997*, edited by Ronald D. Cohen. New York: Routledge, 2005.

Merriam, Alan. *The Anthropology of Music*. Evanston, IL: Northwestern University Press, 1964.

Rhodes, Willard. "Toward a Definition of Ethnomusicology." *American Anthropologist*, 58(3), 1956: 457–463.

Rice, Timothy. *Ethnomusicology: A Very Short Introduction*. Oxford /New York: Oxford University Press, 2014.

Weber, Max. *The Rational and Social Foundations of Music*. Carbondale: Southern Illinois University Press, 1958.

CHAPTER 4

Precursors of Ethno-Organology

Since ethno-organology is an integral part of ethnomusicology, one might assume that like ethnomusicology it originated after World War II. In some respects, this assumption is accurate. However, it is important to recognize that throughout history, various scholars conducted in-depth research on the musical instruments of their own cultures, making them precursors of ethno-organology.

4.1 Sebastian Virdung (1465–?)

Sebastian Virdung, a priest and choir singer, published *Musica getutscht* [Music in German] in Basel, Switzerland (Virdung, 1511). This treatise is the oldest printed work in the West focusing on musical instruments and the first of its kind written in the vernacular, thus making it widely accessible and a model for subsequent treatises.

Unfortunately, the copy we possess is incomplete; the missing pages likely continued instructions on fingerings for the recorder flute, which now make up the final part of the volume, accompanied by a woodcut illustration.

The first page explains that the text is in the vernacular rather than Latin, as was customary for treatises of the 16th century, and mentions that it is a synthesis of a larger future work by Virdung. One may wonder why Virdung mentioned a work yet to be written. A possible explanation is that with the treatise *Musica getutscht* he intended to write a simpler work, not very in-depth or full of technical details, so that it would also be accessible to beginners in music.

The entire text is written as an informal conversation between a fictional character, Andreas Silvanus, and the author. Their relationship appears to be on an equal footing; therefore, we assume that Silvanus is thought of as a colleague rather than a student. The book features a woodcut depicting the two protagonists, Virdung and Silvanus, although the names above the figures are likely reversed (Fig. 2).

Fig. 2 Woodcut, from Virdung, *Musica getutscht*

Virdung divides instruments into three groups: stringed, wind-driven, and metallic or other instruments. Among those he describes and depicts are a lute, which belongs to the stringed category; several recorders and a bagpipe, classified as wind-driven; and drums and bells, which fall under the metallic or other instruments group. While the woodcuts were popular at the time, they do not provide enough details to recreate accurate replicas of ancient instruments today. The reason why the descriptions of the instruments are not precise down to the smallest details, and the images are not meticulously refined, could also be that Virdung, addressing a colleague, implicitly assumes that the latter is already familiar with the instruments mentioned and depicted in the woodcuts. In any case, Virdung's use of the vernacular and focus on the musical instruments of German territories are of central interest to our field of study.

4.2 Martin Agricola (1486-1556)

Martin Sohr, known by the humanist surname Agricola due to his peasant back-ground, served as Cantor at one of the Protestant schools that had been newly established at the time, and published the first edition of *Musica instrumentalis deudsch* [Instrumental Music in German] in the late 1520s (Agricola, 1529). This treatise represents an evolution from Virdung's work, discussing how instruments are held, giving more space to fingerings and tuning of viols, and including more illustrations.

In 1545, Agricola published a second edition of this treatise, with several changes:

- A longer text
- Newly redone fingering tables
- A chapter on organ pipes, including a table on the length and diameter of pipes in a 12-tone chromatic scale
- Diagrams concerning bell scales
- A section on the monochord

As with the 1529 edition, the text of the 1545 edition is also in rhyme, but it additionally includes marginal Latin annotations, likely in response to criticism of the first edition, which found it lacking in scientific rigor (Agricola, 1545).

4.3 Silvestro Ganassi del Fontego (1492-1565)

Silvestro Ganassi, a musician from the Republic of Venice, published *La Regola Rubertina* [Ruberto's Rule] (1542) and *Lettione seconda* [Lesson Two] (1543). *La Regola Rubertina* is dedicated to Ruberto Strozzi, a student of Ganassi, and likely takes its name from him. These two publications are parts of the same work: the first centers on the viola da gamba, defined as "viola darcho tastata" (fretted bowed viola) as its characteristic feature was a fingerboard divided into sections by frets, and the second focuses on the violone.

Ganassi explains the correct posture the musician should assume, starting with the head, which should not change its inclination in relation to the instrument by making overly abrupt movements, not even when performing vibrato or fast-paced pieces. He then describes the position of the viola, held between the legs, the way to grip the bow, its use depending on the difficulties and techniques of the piece, such as pizzicato, vibrato, legato, and the execution of trills by semitone, tone, and thirds. Like Ganassi's other treatises, *La Regola Rubertina* is intended for both beginners and true virtuosos.

La Regola Rubertina also contains important information on the classification of instruments in the viol family as well as their tunings. This work influenced generations of musicians, and today Ganassi is recognized as a pioneer in the codification of viola teaching.

4.4 Ludovico Zacconi (1556-1627)

Zacconi's most important work, *Prattica di musica* [Practice of Music], includes a classification of musical instruments in its fourth book, which divides the instruments into three categories: wind, keyboard, and bowed. This classification criterion was later adopted by Michael Praetorius in his *Syntagma Musicum* [Musical Encyclopedia] (1619). The instruments described and illustrated by Zacconi include: cornetts, violins (it is worth noting that until then the violin had only been used for ballet music), recorders and transverse flutes, crumhorns, bassoons, and trombones.

Zacconi's work is notable for its many drawings, made by Zacconi himself, some of which are difficult to interpret, leading some critics to label them as "musical hieroglyphs" (Wuidar, 2007).

4.5 Vincenzo Giustiniani (1564-1637)

Vincenzo Giustiniani, Marquis of Bassano, is the author of a series of writings on the arts and crafts, in the form of letters addressed to the historian Theodor Ameyden, who had requested them. He discussed various instruments, including "li Flauti, li Piferi, le Viole di conserto e la Viola Doppia o sia Bastarda, il Violino, il Cornetto, il Pifero Tedesco, la Sordellina, la Piva, il Culascione e la Sanfornia" (Flutes, Fifes, Consort Viols and the Double or Bastard Viola, the Violin, the Cornett, the German Fife, the Sordellina, the Piva, the Colascione, and the Jaw Harp) (Giustiniani, 2002 [1628]: 54): he places in a particular group "gli Organi, il Liuto o Pandòra, l'Arpa, il Cimbalo, la Tiorba, Chitarra e Lira; tutti stromenti sopra quali si può cantare ad una o più voci" (the Organs, the Lute or Pandore, the Harp, the Harpsichord, the Theorbo, the Guitar, and the Lyre; all instruments that can accompany one voice or more voices singing polyphonically) (Giustiniani, 2002 [1628]: 54). The colascione, a type of lute with an extremely long neck (which could reach up to two meters in length) that was very common during the period between the 15th and the 17th centuries, the *sordellina* and the piva, both types of Italian bagpipes, and the jaw harp are among the instruments discussed in this book; they will be further explored in Chapters 11, 13, and 14.

4.6 Michael Praetorius (1571–1621)

Michael Praetorius was a German composer and music theorist.

For the field of ethnomusicology, Praetorius's treatise *Syntagma musicum* [Musical compendium], published in three volumes between 1614 and 1619, is highly significant. In addition to the explanatory text, it contains numerous drawings and is regarded as one of the primary sources for studying early Baroque performance practices.

The second volume, titled *De organographia*, despite its Latin title, is written in German and covers all musical instruments, both ancient and modern, with numerous illustrations and includes a highly detailed description of the pipe organ (Praetorius, 1619). This volume being in German suggests that, unlike the more theoretical first and third volumes, which are written in Latin, it was not primarily aimed at musicologists and theorists but rather addressed a wider audience, including performers and, more broadly, music enthusiasts.

4.7 Marin Mersenne (1588–1648)

Philosopher, theologian, scientist, and a member of the Order of Minims, Marin Mersenne authored several theoretical works on music. Among them are *Harmonicorum instrumentorum libri IV* [Four Books on Musical Instruments] published in 1636 (republished in an expanded edition in 1648) and the monumental *Harmonie universelle*, published between 1636 and 1637.

The full title of the *Harmonie universelle* is *Traité de l'harmonie universelle, où est contenu la musique théorique et pratique des anciens et modernes, avec les causes de ses effets, enrichie de raison prise de la philosophie et des mathématiques*

[Treatise on universal harmony, in which is contained the theoretical and practical music of the ancients and moderns, with the causes of its effects, enriched with reasoning drawn from philosophy and mathematics] (Mersenne, 1636–1637). This extensive treatise represents the summa of musical knowledge of that time.

Notably, alongside the *Harmonie universelle*, which is written in French, Mersenne published the treatise *Harmonicorum instrumentorum libri IV*, a shorter work written in Latin (Mersenne, 1636a). This choice was likely driven by the fact that Latin remained the international language of science, understood by scholars who were not native French speakers.

Mersenne's scientific rigor is evident in his descriptions: each instrument is not only described in detail and depicted in illustrations but also measured with precision in all its dimensions, including the diameter of the holes. In his instrument descriptions, Mersenne first explains how the sound is produced. He then explores how, through successive modifications, one instrument evolved into another, as seen, for example, in the transition from the dulcian to the baroque bassoon. Mersenne dedicates particular attention to the *sordellina*, which was previously mentioned in this book in relation to Giustiniani and is discussed in greater detail in Chapter 14. He highlights that the *sordellina* allows for polyphonic playing with two voices, while still being able to produce two drone sounds.

4.8 Athanasius Kircher (1602–1680)

The most important work of the German Jesuit Athanasius Kircher is *Musurgia Universalis sive ars magna consoni et dissoni* [The Universal Musical Art or the Great Art of Consonance and Dissonance], a musical treatise in Latin, comprising 10 books, written between 1644 and 1649 and published in Rome in 1650.

The sixth book of the treatise, titled *De Musica Instrumentali* [Instrumental Music], classifies instruments into three categories: string instruments, wind instruments, and percussion instruments (Kircher, 1650). In the section on wind instruments, there are intriguing illustrations of ancient instruments like the serpent, along with a figure that may possibly depict the pipes and drones of a bagpipe. However, modern scholars, upon analyzing the image, believe that mouthpiece holes, resembling those of recorders, can be observed on the pipes (Crane, 1956), leaving uncertainty as to which instrument the image actually represents.

Kircher will be mentioned again in Chapter 14, in reference to his role as curator of the Museum of the Collegio Romano of the Jesuits, a museum established in 1650.

Among its many curious objects and machines, the exhibition also included musical instruments.

4.9 Charles Burney (1726-1814)

Between 1776 and 1789, the English composer and music historian Charles Burney wrote a significant *General History of Music*, in which he laid the groundwork for comparative musicology. While he followed the common practice of studying classical sources from Greek and Roman writers, Burney introduced an innovative approach by comparing them with studies by non-European authors (Burney, 1776–1789). This enabled him to draw connections between Greco-Roman instruments and those of African and Eastern origins, challenging longstanding myths and legends. For instance, when discussing the aulos and the lyre, instruments referenced in Greek mythology, Burney notes that every culture has invented and developed its own types and models of "flute" [sic]. As for the lyre, he suggests that it was likely invented in Abyssinia, where it has been continuously used since ancient times (Burney, 1776: I).

4.10 Nikolaj Dobroljubov (1836-1861)

The Russian poet and journalist Nikolaj Dobroljubov, who had a background in sociology and politics, was highly critical of Russian society as it was in his time. Motivated by a revolutionary ideology, he believed that to foster the awakening of a people, one must first understand their inner life. Building on this conviction, Dobroljubov developed a keen interest in popular music, both vocal and instrumental, seeing it as a means to uncover what the people thought, the themes that mattered to them, and the stage of their evolution, both technically and sociopolitically (Dobroljubov, 1962 [1857]).

4.11 Béla Bartók (1881-1945)

Beginning in 1867, Austria extended its governance over Hungary, imposing both its administrative control and cultural models. In response to this situation of "foreign cultural domination," many Hungarian intellectuals sought to foster a sense of ethnic and cultural identity among the Hungarian people by exploring the origins of Hungarian poetry and music. Initially, Bartók's interest in folk music aligned with that of his fellow Hungarian intellectuals. However, with the collaboration of composer and linguist Zoltán Kodály, Bartók soon embarked on extensive field research. Using a phonograph, he recorded traditional music not only from Hungarian communities but also from Romanian, Slovak, and Bulgarian minorities living within the country. This systematic research began in 1906–1907 and continued annually, whenever Bartók was free from his teaching duties at the Hungarian Academy of Music. Through this work, Bartók "discovered" that Hungarian folk music was rooted in the pentatonic scale, independent of the major–minor tonal system used in classical music (Nelson, 2012).

During his fieldwork between 1907 and 1914, Bartók's research extended beyond vocal music to include traditional instrumental music. He focused particularly on pieces performed on flute, clarinet, bagpipes, swineherd's horn, and violin (Tari, 2006).

Summary

Over the centuries, various scholars have conducted extensive research on the musical instruments of their own cultures and can thus be regarded as precursors of ethno-organology. Among them are: 1) Sebastian Virdung (1465–?); 2) Martin Agricola (1486–1556); 3) Silvestro Ganassi del Fontego (1492–1565); 4) Ludovico Zacconi (1556–1627); 5) Vincenzo Giustiniani (1564–1637); 6) Michael Praetorius (1571–1621); 7) Marin Mersenne (1588–1648); 8) Athanasius Kircher (1602–1680); 9) Charles Burney (1726–1814); 10) Nikolaj Dobroljubov (1836–1861); 11) Béla Bartók (1881–1945). This chapter highlights, for each scholar, the circumstances that sparked their interest in ethno-organological issues, the works they published on these topics, and their most notable insights—many of which were centuries ahead of contemporary ethnomusicological studies.

Keywords

General History of Music, Harmonicorum Instrumentorum Libri IV, Harmonie Universelle, La Regola Rubertina, Lettione Seconda, Musica Getutscht, Musica Instrumentalis Deudsch, Musurgia Universalis, Prattica di Musica, Syntagma Musicum.

Preeminent Figures

- Athanasius Kircher
- Béla Bartók
- Charles Burney
- Ludovico Zacconi
- Marin Mersenne
- Martin Agricola
- Michael Praetorius
- Nikolaj Dobroljubov
- Sebastian Virdung
- Silvestro Ganassi del Fontego
- Vincenzo Giustiniani

Questions for Review

1. What is the oldest printed treatise on musical instruments in the West?
2. What distinguishes the second edition of *Musica instrumentalis deudsch* from the first edition?
3. Which instruments are covered, respectively, by *La Regola Rubertina* and *Lettione seconda*?
4. Why have the drawings in *Prattica di musica* been described as "musical hieroglyphs"?
5. Which treatise contains Michael Praetorius's *De Organographia*?
6. What characteristics set *Harmonicorum instrumentorum libri IV* apart from *Harmonie universelle*?
7. Which treatise includes Athanasius Kircher's *De Musica Instrumentali*?
8. In what ways did Charles Burney lay the groundwork for comparative musicology?
9. Which instruments were the focus of Béla Bartók's ethnomusicological studies?

Further Reading and Online Resources

Agricola, Martin. *Musica instrumentalis deudsch*. Wittenberg, Germany: Georg Rhaw, 1529.

Agricola, Martin. *Musica instrumentalis deudsch*, 2nd edition. Wittenberg, Germany: Georg Rhaw, 1545.

Burney, Charles. *A General History of Music,* I: London, 1776, II: London, 1782, III: London, 1789, IV. London, 1789.

Crane, Frederick Baron. "Athanasius Kircher, Musurgia Universalis (Rome, 1650): The Section on Musical Instruments." Iowa Research Online, 1956. Accessed November 3, 2024. https://iro.uiowa.edu/esploro/outputs/9983776780602771.

Dobroljubov, Nikolaj. *Sobranie sočinenij* [Collected Works], III, edited by B. I. Bursov, Moscow: Goslitizdat, 1962 (1857).

Ganassi del Fontego, Silvestro. *La Regola Rubertina.* Venetia, 1542.

Ganassi del Fontego, Silvestro. *Lettione Seconda.* Venetia, 1543.

Giustiniani, Vincenzo. "Discorso sopra la musica dei suoi tempi (1628)." *Informazione Organistica*, XIV, 2002: 43–56.

Kircher, Athanasius. *Musurgia universalis sive ars magna consoni et dissoni,* VI: *Musica organica sive De musica instrumentali.* Roma: Ex Typographia Haeredum Francisci Corbelletti, 1650.

Mersenne, Marin. *Harmonicorum instrumentorum libri IV*. Lutetiae Parisiorum (Paris): Gvillielmi Bavdry, 1636 (1636a)

Mersenne, Marin. *Harmonie Universelle, contenant la theorie et la pratique de la musique, où il est traité de la Nature des Sons & des Mouvemens, des Consonances, des Dissonances, des Genres, des Modes, de la Composition, de la Voix, des Chants, & de toutes sortes d'Instrumens Harmoniques.* Paris: Sebastien Cramoisy, 1636 (1636b).

Mersenne, Marin. *Seconde partie de l'harmonie universelle: contenant la pratique des consonances, & des dissonances dans le contrepoint figuré, la methode d'enseigner, & d'apprendre à chanter, l'embellissement des airs, la musique accentuelle, la rythmique, la prosodie, & la metrique françoise, la maniere de chanter les odes de Pindare, & d'Horace, l'utilité de l'harmonie, & plusieurs nouvelles observations, tant physiques que mathématiques: avec deux tables, l'une des propositions, & l'autre des matieres.* Paris: Pierre Ballard, 1637.

Nelson, David Taylor. "Béla Bartók: The Father of Ethnomusicology." *Musical Offerings*, 3(2), 2012: 75–91.

Praetorius, Michael. *Syntagma musicum*, II: *De organographia*. Wolfenbüttel, Germany: Elias Holwein, 1619.

Tari, Lujza. "Bartók's Collection of Hungarian Instrumental Folk Music and Its System." *Studia Musicologica*, 47(2) June 2006: 141–166.

Virdung, Sebastian. *Musica getuscht*. Basel, Switzerland, 1511.

Wuidar, Laurence. "Les 'Geroglifici Musicali' du Padre Zacconi." *Revue Belge de Musicologie*, 2007: 61–87.

CHAPTER 5

Accounts of Travelers

Chapter 4 delved into the early pioneers of ethno-organological studies who were active in Italy and throughout Europe. In contrast, Chapter 5 shifts its focus to individuals who, over time, while not strictly ethno-organologists, have provided insights into the musical instruments and practices of southern Italy.

For centuries prior to the invention of the phonograph around 1877, musical instruments served as the primary portable artifacts capable of preserving and sharing global music traditions. This often compelled "great travelers"—those venturing into distant lands—to acquire typical instruments during their journeys, sometimes evolving into avid collectors themselves.

Beyond mere acquisition, some travelers provided detailed descriptions of these instruments and their usage, whereas others illustrated them through sketches in their letters and diaries. Professional painters among them went further, producing full-fledged paintings. These artistic representations varied in approach: sketches aimed at straightforward documentation, while paintings blended reality with fantastical elements to evoke exotic and fairy-tale-like travel experiences.

Another facet of travel was exemplified by colonizers—populations who migrated from their homelands to establish settlements in new territories. Colonizers typically brought with them musical instruments from their motherland or crafted new ones in their new homes. These instruments were tied to the culture of the motherland, including its myths and religious beliefs.

In antiquity, southern Italy was first the destination of travelers and merchants from Greece and later, starting from the 8th century BCE, the object of Greek colonization. Significant portions of Campania, Basilicata, and Calabria became known as Magna Graecia, where musical instruments imported from the Greek homeland were employed, eventually becoming integral to the traditional instruments of those regions.

Between the 9th and the 11th centuries, Sicily was invaded and conquered by Arabs and Berbers, marking a period of Islamic domination (827–1072). Arab travelers who visited Sicily during this era provided valuable insights into the instruments used, sometimes explicitly noting that certain instruments were imported from North Africa, such as various types of oboes and drums (Amari, 1880).

In both the Greek colonization of Southern Italy and the Islamic rule over Sicily, it is plausible that the construction of new instruments locally involved a fusion of new construction techniques with methods already established in those regions, resulting in instruments characterized by hybrid features.

From the 18th century onward, it became fashionable for the offspring of wealthy European aristocrats to embark on the Grand Tour—a lengthy journey lasting a year or more, spanning Europe with Italy as a prominent destination. These travelers often lingered in various Italian cities for extended periods.

In the final three decades of the 18th century, Sicily was "discovered" by European intellectuals. Influenced by their classical education and imbued with ideological and aesthetic values, these travelers frequently depicted the island as a timeless natural paradise in their descriptions. Music played a defining role in scenes of relaxation and leisure, often intertwined with dance, highlighting its sensual qualities.

For example, the Frenchman Jean-Pierre Houël (1735–1813), while passing near Sciacca (in present-day Agrigento province) between 1770 and 1776, remarked, "Rural music holds a distinct charm; there is a type of ancient flute, already depicted in certain bas-reliefs portraying Bacchanalia" (cited in Tuzet, 1955: 284–285). Bacchanalia were festivals honoring Bacchus, the Roman equivalent of the Dionysian celebrations in ancient Greece.

Similarly, toward the late 1700s, in his work *Briefe über Kalabrien und Sizilien* [Letters on Calabria and Sicily], the German Johann Heinrich Bartels (1761–1850) noted that Calabrian music "enchants travelers who fall into a sort of Dionysian trance" (cited in Tuzet, 1955: 285).

Another German traveler, Joseph Hager (1757–1819), succinctly described Sicilian folk songs as "amorous and playful in character" in his 1799 work titled *Gemälde von Palermo* [Paintings of Palermo] (Hager, 1799: 48).

Jean-Pierre Houël, previously mentioned, was a professional painter who published the four volumes of his work *Voyage pittoresque des îles de Sicile, Malte et Lipari* [Picturesque voyage of the islands of Sicily, Malta, and Lipari] between 1782 and 1787. This collection comprises 264 illustrated plates, with

Plate 182 depicting an exterior view of the "Ear of Dionysius" cave in Syracuse. In this illustration, men are shown demonstrating the echo phenomenon—for which the Ear of Dionysius is known since ancient times—by generating loud noises through rifle shots, and vigorously playing a large shoulder drum and a trumpet (Houël, 1782–1787) (Fig. 3).

Fig. 3 Houël, *Voyage pittoresque*, plate 182

The visual artist Louis-Jean Desprès (1743–1804) created many images for Jean-Claude Richard, Abbot of Saint-Non's (1727–1791) work *Voyage pittoresque ou description des Royaumes de Naples et de Sicile* [Picturesque voyage or description of the kingdoms of Naples and Sicily], published in four volumes from 1781 to 1786. One plate in the fourth volume depicts a *piffero* player performing alongside a player of the *zampogna a chiave* (southern Italian bagpipe with key). Another plate portrays a rural scene near the Greek theater of Syracuse, where amidst grazing cows and donkeys, two musicians—a piffero player and a frame drum player—are performing music. A man and a woman are dancing to the rhythms of this music (de Saint-Non, 1785) (Fig. 4).

Fig. 4 de Saint-Non, *Voyage pittoresque*, Dancers moving to the sound of a *piffero* and a frame drum

In the summer of 1816, the German musician Giacomo Meyerbeer (1791–1864) spent a vacation in Sicily. While he did not provide detailed descriptions of musical instruments, he documented 38 pieces of Sicilian songs and dances, detailing their contexts and performance styles (Bose, 1993).

The Frenchman Auguste de Sayve (1790–1854), in his work *Voyage en Sicile. Fait en 1820 et 1821* [Journey to Sicily. Made in 1820 and 1821], published the following year, described the double cane flute (de Sayve, 1822).

Another Frenchman, Louis de Forbin (1777–1841), begins his travel account *Souvenirs de la Sicile* [Memories of Sicily], published in 1823, with an image depicting a dance occurring in the Greco-Roman theater of Taormina. In this scene, two dancers move to the rhythm of a frame drum, observed by a kneeling man and a woman reclining on the ground. The classical ambience is set by the theater, while foreground shrubs and trees add naturalistic elements (de Forbin, 1823) (Fig. 5).

Fig. 5 de Forbin, *Souvenirs de la Sicile*, Dance to the sound of a frame drum

An English traveler, the painter Arthur John Strutt (1818–1888), also traveled to Sicily. In his narratives included in the volume *A Pedestrian Tour in Calabria and Sicily* (1842), he vividly describes the procession of the Immaculate Conception that he witnessed in Palermo in December 1841. During this event, Strutt observed and listened to bagpipes and frame drums. He noted that bagpipes were characterized by their large size and specific construction materials, whereas frame drums were described as having a small size, jingles, and no membrane. Strutt also provided illustrations detailing the playing technique, explaining that frame drums were held by the performer with the right hand and struck against the forearm and wrist of the left hand (Strutt, 1842).

Summary

For many centuries, before the invention of the phonograph in 1877, musical instruments were the only easily transportable objects that could preserve and convey the music of the world. This often inspired "great travelers," those who ventured into distant lands, to acquire typical instruments from the places they visited, and in some cases, become collectors. Beyond merely purchasing these instruments, some travelers provided detailed descriptions of the instruments and their uses, sketched them in their letters and diaries, and professional painters among them created full-scale paintings. This chapter highlights notable travelers who documented popular instruments and the occasions of their use, including Jean-Pierre Houël (1735–1813), Johann Heinrich Bartels (1761–1850), Joseph Hager (1757–1819), Jean-Claude Richard, Abbot of Saint-Non (1727–1791), Giacomo Meyerbeer (1791–1864), Auguste de Sayve (1790–1854), Louis de Forbin (1777–1841), and Arthur John Strutt (1818–1888).

Keywords

Grand Tour, Great Travelers, Greek Colonization of Southern Italy, Greek Theater, Islamic Domination of Sicily, Procession, Rural Scene.

Preeminent Figures

- Arthur John Strutt
- Auguste de Sayve
- Giacomo Meyerbeer
- Jean-Claude Richard, Abbot of Saint-Non, known as de Saint-Non
- Jean-Pierre Houël
- Johann Heinrich Bartels
- Joseph Hager
- Louis de Forbin
- Louis-Jean Desprès

Questions for Review

1. What types of travelers documented musical instruments from cultures different from their own?

2. When did the Greek colonization of southern Italy begin?
3. Which peoples conquered Sicily between the 9th and the11th centuries?
4. What was the Grand Tour?
5. What historical significance do sketches and paintings of musical instruments hold?
6. What distinguishes the descriptions of instruments related to southern Italy in the works of de Forbin, de Saint-Non, and Houël?

Further Reading and Online Resources

Amari, Michele. *Biblioteca arabo-sicula*. Torino, Italy/Roma: Ermanno Loescher, 1880.

Bartels, Johann Heinrich. *Briefe über Kalabrien und Sizilien*, 3 vols. Göttingen, Germany: Dietrich. 1787–1791.

Bose, Fritz. *Musiche popolari siciliane raccolte da Giacomo Meyerbeer*. Palermo, Italy: Sellerio, 1993.

de Forbin, Louis. *Souvenirs de la Sicile*. Paris: Imprimerie Royale, 1823.

de Saint-Non, Jean Claude Richard. *Voyage pittoresque ou description des Royaumes de Naples et de Sicile*, 4 vols., IV: *Quatrième volume, contenant la description de la Sicile* (1785), Paris, 1781–1786.

de Sayve, Auguste. *Voyage en Sicile. Fait en 1820 et 1821*, 3 vols. Paris: Bertrand, 1822.

Hager, Joseph, *Gemälde von Palermo*. Berlin: Heinrich Frölich, 1799.

Houël, Jean Pierre. *Voyage pittoresque des îles de Sicile, Malte et Lipari*, 4 vols. Paris: Imprimerie de Monsieur, 1782–1787.

Strutt, Arthur John. *A Pedestrian Tour in Calabria and Sicily*. London: Newby, 1842.

Tuzet, Hélène. *La Sicile au XVIIIe siècle vue par les voyageurs étrangers*. Strasbourg, France: P.H. Heitz, 1955.

CHAPTER 6

Migration of Musical Instruments

As discussed in Chapter 4 (section 4.9), the English scholar Charles Burney is mentioned for comparing what was narrated in ancient myths, such as the Greek myths about the origins of the aulos and the lyre, with what was revealed by the discoveries of ancient instruments. This led him to propose that the lyre was originally invented in Abyssinia (modern-day Ethiopia) and later introduced to Europe, where it underwent further development (Burney, 1789).

The construction of a musical instrument is influenced by the stage of development that material technology has reached at that time. For example, until the mid-1600s, stringed instruments used strings made from animal gut. Around the mid-1600s, it became feasible to produce strings with a gut core thinly wrapped in metal. These "spun strings" were heavier but did not significantly increase in thickness. They had two main characteristics: increased sound power due to their weight and the ability to provide a quick attack and agility in performance, thanks to their relatively unchanged thickness.

The introduction of these new types of spun strings allowed for a blend of sound power and performance agility, facilitating innovations in compositions for bowed instruments. Therefore, advancements in material technologies prompted changes in instruments, enabled new compositional styles, and influenced emerging aesthetic concepts.

Ethno-organology examines the diverse contexts in which instruments are utilized, including dance, rituals, celebratory events such as weddings and births, solemn occasions like funerals, civic celebrations, and more. One of the roles of ethno-organology is to investigate the specific cultural settings where musical instruments are employed.

Burney emphasized that, despite being regarded as a pivotal instrument in the musical traditions of Greeks and Romans, the lyre actually originated in Africa. Throughout history, musical instruments have often been transported to distant contexts from their place of origin, owing to the relative ease of their long-distance transportation.

What happens when a musical instrument is introduced to a new environment? The instrument gradually comes to be played by performers who are not native to its original culture. These performers perceive the instrument "with fresh eyes," free from the constraints of fidelity to the instrument's original cultural context. Over time, these performers are likely to make adaptations to the instrument, while further alterations may be introduced by new craftsmen. These modifications foster the development of new performance techniques and aesthetic concepts, facilitating an exchange—both ways—between the instrument's culture of origin and the new culture that embraces it.

Indeed, even when instruments from distant locations share similarities, there remain organological and performative differences that stem from variations in aesthetic and musical concepts (Magnusson, 2021).

Summary

This chapter explores what happens when an instrument is introduced to a different culture. As the instrument begins to be played by performers outside of its culture of origin, they may view and use it in ways that are not bound by the traditions of its original context. Consequently, these performers and new instrument makers often introduce modifications to the instrument. These changes, in turn, lead to the development of new playing techniques and aesthetic concepts, fostering an exchange between the instrument's original culture and the new culture that adopts it.

When similarities are observed between instruments from distant regions, they are often accompanied by differences in construction, function, and performance, reflecting variations in aesthetic concepts.

Keywords

Cultural Context in Which an Instrument Is Used, Exchanges Between the Instrument's Culture of Origin and Its Destination Culture, Material Technology, Organological and Performative Differences Related to Variations in Aesthetic and Musical Concepts

Preeminent Figures

- Charles Burney
- Thor Magnusson

Questions for Review

1. How important is the stage of material technology development in the process of constructing an instrument?
2. What modifications might be made to an instrument by performers outside the culture of its origin?
3. What is the relationship between an instrument's construction techniques, playing techniques, and aesthetic concepts?

Further Reading and Online Resources

Burney, Charles. *A General History of Music,* I: London 1776, II: London, 1782, III: London, 1789, IV: London, 1789.

Magnusson, Thor. "The Migration of Musical Instruments: On the Socio-Technological Conditions of Musical Evolution." *Journal of New Music Research*, 50(2), 2021: 175–183.

CHAPTER 7

Classifications of Musical Instruments

In Chapter 4, several precursors of ethno-organological studies were introduced. Among them, Silvestro Ganassi del Fontego, in his work *La Regola Rubertina* (1542), undertook a classification of musical instruments with a particular focus on viols. Similarly, Athanasius Kircher, in his *Musurgia Universalis* (1649), presented a comprehensive classification of musical instruments. Both scholars emphasized the importance of systematically studying musical instruments, analyzing similarities and differences to establish criteria for grouping them into coherent categories.

Indeed, not only these theorists, but every civilization and culture has developed its own system for classifying musical instruments. However, the process of classification—dividing instruments into coherent groups based on specific criteria—is inherently complex. This complexity can stem from various elements, including philosophical and religious considerations, with multiple logical criteria often employed.

Some of the most noteworthy classification systems include those from Chinese and Indian traditions, the system used by the Aré Aré people (a population residing in the Solomon Islands), as well as those developed by Victor-Charles Mahillon, Hornbostel-Sachs, and André Schaeffner.

7.1 The Chinese System

This system is likely the oldest known instrument classification system, dating back to around 2300 BCE. Instruments are categorized into eight groups based on the primary material used in their construction: stone, metal, silk, bamboo, wood, leather, gourds, and terracotta. It is important to note, however, that these materials, which form the basis of the classification, hold greater symbolic significance in relation to Chinese philosophy than actual musical value based on timbral differences among the groups.

While the system appears to be founded on objective observations about the materials used in instrument construction, a closer examination reveals that this distinction is closely linked to Chinese cultural beliefs and may seem arbitrary to those unfamiliar with its cultural context (Desjacques, 2011).

7.2 The Indian System

Found in an encyclopedic treatise from the 5th century BCE, the Indian system diverges completely from mythological and metaphysical concepts, focusing instead on the physical properties of materials that influence how instruments produce sound. It classifies instruments into four main categories:

1. String instruments,
2. Membrane instruments,
3. Wind instruments, and
4. Percussion instruments other than drums.

Scholars believe that this systematic approach influenced European classifications of the late 19th and the early 20th centuries (Desjacques, 2011).

7.3 The Aré Aré People's System

The Aré Aré people, who inhabit the Solomon Islands archipelago, classify their instruments based on the different types of music produced:

- Music produced on bamboo instruments, whether blown into, struck, or rubbed (e.g., with a bow);
- Rhythms created on wooden drums;
- Sound activities involving water;
- Human vocalization accompanied by musical instruments (Desjacques, 2011).

7.4 European Classification Systems

7.4.1 The Victor-Charles Mahillon Classification

Victor-Charles Mahillon (1841–1924) was the founder and first curator of the Musical Instrument Museum at the Brussels Conservatory of Music. In 1893, he recognized that the conventional classification of instruments used in orchestras (strings, woodwinds, brass instruments, percussion instruments) was inadequate for categorizing all the world's instruments into cohesive classes.

Mahillon turned to the Indian system for inspiration, asking the question: What vibrating material produces the sound? Guided by the principle that different timbres are produced through the vibration of different materials, he identified:

- **Autophones:** Instruments that produce sound through their own vibration.
- **Membranophones:** Instruments with membranes that produce sound through direct or indirect percussion or friction.
- **Chordophones:** Instruments with strings that produce sound through plucking, bowing, etc.
- **Aerophones:** Instruments where sound is produced by vibrating air (Mahillon, 1880–1892).

7.4.2 The Hornbostel-Sachs Classification

Introduced in 1914 in the article "Systematik der Musikinstrumente. Ein Versuch" [Classification of Musical Instruments: An Attempt] in the *Zeitschrift für Ethnologie* [Journal of Ethnology], and subsequently translated into English (von Hornbostel and Sachs, 1961), this classification by musicologist and ethnomusicologist Erich von Hornbostel (1877–1935) and musicologist Curt Sachs (1881–1959) categorizes instruments into four classes based on the material that vibrates, like Mahillon's approach. Sachs and Hornbostel employed more "scientific" terminology:

- **Chordophones:** All string instruments, regardless of how vibration is initiated (plucking, bowing, etc.).
- **Membranophones:** Instruments with one or two membranes set into vibration directly or indirectly through percussion or friction.
- **Aerophones:** Instruments where vibrating air produces sound, including those where an object rotated in the surrounding air causes vibration (e.g., the bullroarer), single- or double-reed instruments, and those where the performer's lips vibrate (e.g., the trumpet).
- **Idiophones:** This class encompasses all the instruments that do not belong to the previous classes: this class includes instruments made from relatively rigid materials (wood, bamboo, horn, metal, stone, glass, etc.), distinguishing them from instruments made from more elastic materials

(like strings and membranes) or instruments where air vibrates (von Hornbostel and Sachs, 1914).

7.4.3 The André Schaeffner Classification

In the early 1930s, André Schaeffner (1895–1980) developed his own classification system, dividing instruments into two main groups (Schaeffner, 1931):

- **Solid Vibrating Body Instruments:** This group can be subdivided into two sub-classes:
    - i) Instruments with a solid body not susceptible to tension, very rigid, and with an indeterminate pitch (examples include stone or wooden bars, shells, bones, metal instruments, and glass instruments).
    - ii) Instruments where the vibrating solid body is flexible or susceptible to tension, producing sounds of varying pitch, such as piano strings, harp strings, and membranophones.
- **Air Vibration Instruments (Aerophones):** This group can be further divided into:
    - i) Instruments where ambient air vibrates (such as the bullroarer);
    - ii) Instruments where an air column vibrates, with distinctions such as:
        - a) Non-reed instruments, such as the flute and the ocarina;
        - b) Instruments where the performer's lips vibrate, like the trumpet, the trombone, and the horn;
        - c) Single-reed (e.g., the clarinet) or double-reed instruments (e.g., the oboe).

7.5 Revisions and Applications

As evidenced above, every classification system follows criteria that are logical within the culture that expresses them but may appear illogical to those outside that culture. Some cultures emphasize connections to philosophical or religious principles, while others base their classification solely on concrete elements, such as the materials used to construct the instruments, the method used to induce sound production, and so on.

Drawing on:

- a) The classification revised by the Musical Instrument Museums Online (MIMO) Consortium, which provides information on collections of musical instruments preserved in public museums worldwide (MIMO Consortium, 2011);

b) The revision of the Hornbostel–Sachs classification by Febo Guizzi (von Hornbostel, Sachs, and Guizzi, 2020); and

c) Gian Nicola Spanu's classification of Sardinian instruments (Spanu, 1994),

it is possible to identify several groupings of instruments that will be the focus of Chapters 8, 9, 11–15:

1. **Idiophones**

   Idiophones are instruments where the material of the instrument body or a part thereof emits sound by its own elasticity or rigidity without the need for tensioned membranes or strings. Idiophones include concussion idiophones, shaken idiophones, struck idiophones, scraped idiophones, and plucked idiophones.

   A) **Concussion Idiophones:** Instruments in which two or more solid components, designed to sound together, are struck against each other. Clappers are a typical example (Fig. 6).

Fig. 6 Clapper

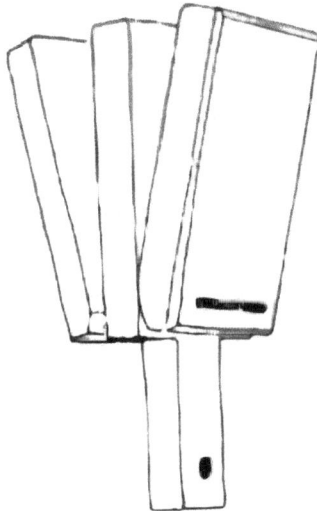

   B) **Shaken Idiophones:** Instruments that produce sound when small loose elements inside or attached to the instrument impact its body due to shaking motion. Sistra belong to this category (Fig. 7).

Fig. 7 Sistrum

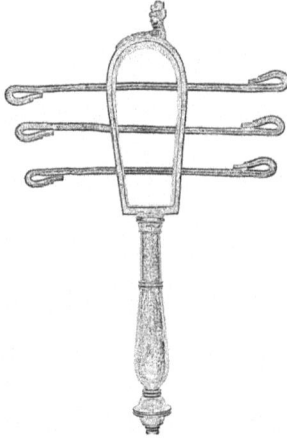

C) **Struck Idiophones:** Instruments that generate sound when they are directly hit, causing the instrument itself to vibrate as the primary sound source. Among these, percussion vessels are a distinct type, characterized by a hollow, resonant body shaped like a container. Bells, where the non-resonant device is the clapper or striker, fall into this group (Fig. 8).

Fig. 8 Bell

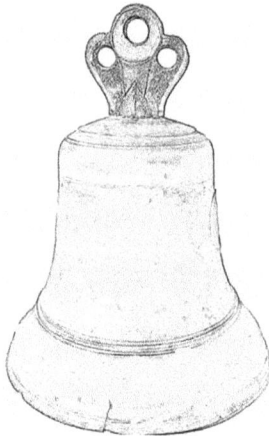

D) **Scraped Idiophones:** These instruments create sound when a non-resonant object is moved across a grooved surface, producing repeated

percussive contacts, or when an elastic sound-producing element inter-
acts with a textured non-resonant body in a similar fashion. Ratchets
exemplify this category: they feature a toothed wheel with an axle
as a handle and a flexible board that strikes against the wheel's teeth
when rotated by the performer (Fig. 9).

Fig. 9 Ratchet

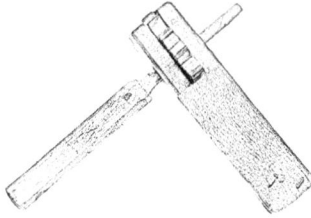

E) **Plucked Idiophones:** Instruments that produce sound through small
elastic plates (lamellae) fixed at one end. When bent and released, these
plates vibrate as they return to their original position. A well-known
example is the jaw harp (Fig. 10).

Fig. 10 Jaw harp

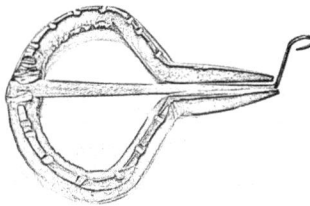

2. **Membranophones**
Membranophones are instruments whose vibrating bodies are membranes
under tension. Two important sub-classes are as follows.

A) **Struck membranophones:** Instruments in which the membranes are
struck: examples include cylindrical drums, which can be single-headed or
double-headed, meaning they have one or two membranes (Fig. 11), and
frame drums. In the latter, the height of the body of the instrument does not
exceed the radius of the membrane. In the European context, tambourines,
which are single-headed frame drums, are common (Fig. 12)

Fig. 11 Cylindrical drum

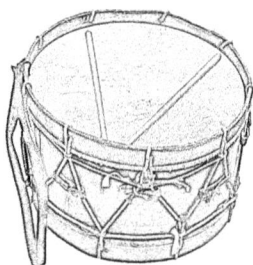

Fig. 12 Frame drum

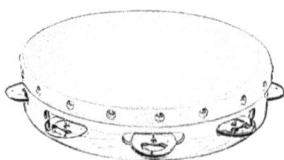

B) Friction Drums: Among these are indirect friction drums, in which the performer manipulates a stick or a string that transmits the impulse to the membrane of the instrument (Fig. 13). An example is the *putipù*, also known by other names, including *bufù* and *bbù-bbù*.

Fig. 13 Friction drum

3. **Chordophones**

    Chordophones are instruments in which one or more strings are stretched between fixed points. In the sub-class of composite chordophones, the instrument consists of a support for the strings and a resonator that are organically connected and cannot be separated without destroying the sound apparatus. This sub-class includes lutes, among which the colascione is used in traditional and folk music (Fig. 14).

Fig. 14 Colascione

4. **Acrophones**

    Aerophones are instruments in which air is the primary medium set into vibration. Among these, there are two major sub-classes: free aerophones and wind instruments in the proper sense.

    A) **Free Aerophones:** Free aerophones are instruments in which the vibrating air is not confined within the instrument. Among these are instruments where the airflow is periodically interrupted. An example of a free aerophone where the airflow is periodically interrupted is the bullroarer, an instrument that is swung circularly in the air, generating a deep sound (Fig. 15).

Fig. 15 Bullroarer

Among the free aerophones where the airflow is periodically interrupted, there are some in which the airflow is forced against a series of free reeds, and which are equipped with a bellows to supply the air. This group includes the diatonic accordion and the bandoneon (Fig. 16).

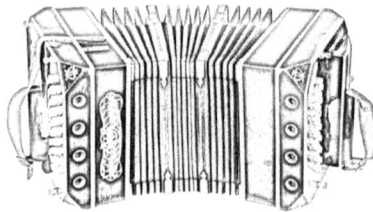

Fig. 16 Bandoneon

B) **Wind Instruments Proper:** These are instruments where the vibrating air is contained within the instrument. This sub-class includes:
1) Edge instruments, where a ribbon-like flow of air strikes against a sharp edge: among these are straight flutes or recorder flutes, in which the performer blows into the upper opening of the tube (Fig. 17).

Fig. 17 Straight flute

2) Reedpipes: here, oscillating blades (called reeds) attached to the instrument allow airflow to intermittently enter the air column setting it into vibration. Among these reedpipes are the instruments in the oboe family, that is, instruments whose pipe is equipped with a double reed, made of two blades that vibrate against each other: the aulos, and the *ciaramella* (this

term understood as a reedpipe) (Fig. 18). Among the reedpipes are also instruments equipped with single reeds, such as the clarinet and the launeddas (Fig. 19).

Fig. 18 Ciaramella

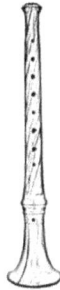

Fig. 19 Launeddas

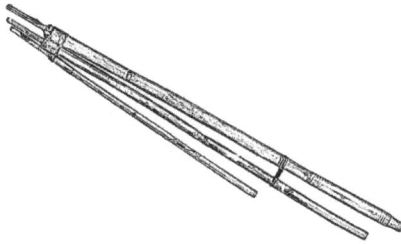

Bagpipes are also part of the reedpipe category and are classified differently depending on whether the pipes use single reeds, double reeds, or a combination of both. For example, the bagpipe called *müsa* is a composite aerophone that has:

1) a conical-bore pipe (chanter) with a double reed (thus analogous to the oboe), equipped with finger holes;
2) a cylindrical-bore pipe (drone) with a single reed (thus analogous to the clarinet), equipped with small finger holes that can be left open or closed, allowing the pedal note to be varied.

Moreover, the pipes are powered by the airflow from a flexible reservoir, called a bag or a sack, which is common to both (Fig. 20).

Fig. 20 Müsa

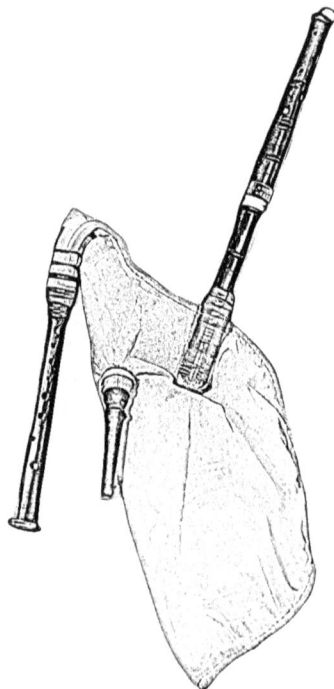

3) Labrosones are instruments in which the performer's breath causes the air column to vibrate, with the lips acting as a vibrating mechanism. One example of a labrosone is the conch shell trumpet (MIMO Consortium, 2011) (Fig. 21).

Fig. 21 Conch shell trumpet

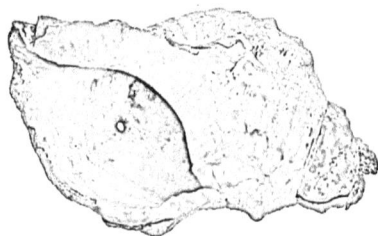

Summary

Every civilization and culture has developed its own system for classifying musical instruments. However, this task—dividing instruments into homogeneous groups based on specific criteria—is complex, as it often involves philosophical, religious, and various logical considerations.

Some of the most notable classification systems include the Chinese, Indian, and Aré Aré people's systems (the Aré Aré are a population from the Solomon Islands archipelago), as well as those developed by Victor-Charles Mahillon, Hornbostel-Sachs, and André Schaeffner. The chapter also explores revisions of the Hornbostel-Sachs classification proposed by the Musical Instrument Museums Online (MIMO) consortium in 2011, Febo Guizzi in 2020, and Gian Nicola Spanu in 1994.

Keywords

Aerophones, Aré Aré People's Classification System, Autophones, Chinese Classification System, Chordophones, European Classification Systems, Idiophones, Indian Classification System, Membranophones, Musical Instrument Museums Online (MIMO), System of Classifying Musical Instruments.

Preeminent Figures

- André Schaeffner
- Curt Sachs
- Erich von Hornbostel
- Febo Guizzi
- Gian Nicola Spanu
- MIMO Consortium
- Victor-Charles Mahillon

Questions for Review

1. What are the main non-European systems for classifying musical instruments?

2. What are the main European systems for classifying musical instruments?
3. In what way can it be said that Mahillon's classification was inspired by the Indian system?
4. What is the main difference between Mahillon's classification and the Hornbostel–Sachs system?
5. How is Schaeffner's classification organized?
6. Which instruments are representative of concussion idiophones, shaken idiophones, struck idiophones, scraped idiophones, and plucked idiophones?
7. What are the main sub-classes of membranophones?
8. How is the class of aerophones structured?

Further Reading and Online Resources

Desjacques, Alain. "La matière et le son: considérations ethnomusicologiques sur les classifications instrumentales." *OpenEdition Journals*, 11, 2011. https://journals.openedition.org/methodos/2508?lang=en

Ganassi del Fontego, Silvestro. *La Regola Rubertina*, Venetia, 1542. Kircher, Athanasius. *Musurgia universalis sive ars magna consoni et dissoni*, VI: *Musica organica sive De musica instrumentali,* Roma, Ex Typographia Haeredum Francisci Corbelletti, 1650.

Mahillon, Victor-Charles. *Catalogue descriptif et analytique du Musée instrumental du Conservatoire royal de musique de Bruxelles*. Ghent, Belgium: Hoste, 1880–1892.

MIMO Consortium. "Revision of the Hornbostel-Sachs Classification of Musical Instruments by the MIMO Consortium." 2011. Accessed November 3, 2024. https://www.passeidireto.com/arquivo/59517844/revision-of-the-hornbostel-sachs-classification-of-musical-instruments-by-the-mi.

Schaeffner, André. "Projet d'une classification nouvelle des instruments de musique." *Bulletin du Musique d'Ethnographie du Trocadéro*, 1(1) 1931: 21–25.

Spanu, Gian Nicola. "Gli strumenti della musica popolare nell'arte sarda." In *Sonos: strumenti della musica popolare sarda*, edited by Gian Nicola Spanu, 27–33. Nuoro, Italy: ISRE Ilisso Edizioni, 1994.

von Hornbostel, Erich Maria, and Curt Sachs. "Systematik der Musikinstrumente. Ein Versuch." 4–5 *Zeitschrift für Ethnologie*, 1914: 553–590.

von Hornbostel, Erich Maria, and Curt Sachs. "Classification of Musical Instruments." Translated from the Original German by Anthony Baines and Klaus P. Wachsmann, *The Galpin Society Journal*, 14, Mar. 1961: 3–29.

von Hornbostel, Erich, Curt Sachs, and Febo Guizzi. "Classification of Musical Instruments." Translated by Anthony Baines and Klaus Wachmann. In *Reflecting on Hornbostel-Sachs's Versuch a Century Later: Proceedings of the International Meeting Venice, July 3–4, 2015*, edited by Cristina Ghirardini, 227–279. Venezia, Italy: Edizioni Fondazione Levi, 2020.

PART 2

Analogies Between Archaeological Finds and Modern Instruments

CHAPTER 8

Instruments from Before the Common Era (BCE)

In Chapter 1, ethno-organology was defined as the study and reflection on musical instruments in traditional music. The term *traditional* stems from *tradition*, which refers to the transmission of customs, practices, memories, and testimonies from one generation to another over time. Therefore, tracing this path back through generations can extend far into the past. As discussed in Chapter 1, ethnology, which is closely connected to ethno-organology, explores themes associated with a group of people, whether large or small, who share the same nation, tribe, or race, and hence the same culture.

At this point, it is essential to consider what is meant by *culture*. In a narrow sense, culture refers to the intellectual development of an individual, encompassing knowledge of literature, history, art, and more. In a broader sense, culture refers to the collective ways in which a particular community addresses its existential challenges. Understandably, once effective solutions to life's fundamental problems (such as obtaining food, building shelters, and maintaining social order) are discovered, these methods are passed down and taught to younger generations over time.

We can imagine that the strategies for addressing fundamental problems depend on various factors, such as:

1. **Climate**.
2. **Orographic Configuration**: The physical landscape of the territory.
3. **Hydrographic Elements**: The presence, position, and consistency of water bodies like seas, lakes, and rivers. Consistency is crucial, as some rivers may flow vigorously during the rainy season but dry up at other times. The availability of water often requires vital decisions for the community.
4. **Community Composition**: The size and demographic makeup of the community (e.g., a community with more young adults may take more decisive actions than one with a larger population of elderly individuals and children).

History demonstrates that a community's needs can evolve over time. On the other hand, while needs evolve and the problems to be addressed change, along with the strategies to solve them, it is likely that certain needs remain constant over time. Ethnologists have studied how populations have solved their existential problems by examining various artifacts created and used over time, now preserved in museums. These include tools, pottery, ornaments, clothing, weapons, and more. Such objects provide valuable insights into how these groups lived, what they believed in, and the ceremonies they performed.

Earlier, we defined culture as the collective ways in which a community addresses its existential challenges. However, what is meant by *religion*?

In essence, religion can be described as a set of beliefs, norms, and ritual practices adhered to by a community. Similar to cultural studies, the study of religion often involves examining artifacts such as utensils used in religious rites (e.g., the aspergillum in Catholicism for sprinkling holy water), pottery (e.g., cruets used during Mass), ornaments, and clothing (e.g., various types of chasubles and stoles worn by priests during the Mass).

These considerations lead us to observe that culture and religion share several characteristics and functions. A scholar argues that religion is, in fact, a part of culture (Roy, 2010). For this reason, music and musical instruments are often integral to both the culture of a group and the religion they follow, as well as to the various religious functions they participate in.

An essential aspect of a group's religion and culture is how they honor the deceased, with specific ceremonies and designated burial places. Often, from the paintings that adorned tombs and the objects placed within them, we can glean valuable insights into the culture and religion of a particular population.

Consider the Etruscan tombs: Etruscan tombs are mentioned here because they are better known, largely due to written records in addition to archaeological findings, but similar burial practices existed among other ancient cultures as well. Tombs were conceived as the new homes of the deceased and were therefore equipped with clothing, ornaments, everyday objects, and supplies of food and drink for their use. Additionally, musical instruments and sound-producing objects were often placed in these tombs.

Among the sources that testify to ancient musical practices, there are not only musical instruments in the strict sense. In addition to the instruments themselves, depictions found in vase paintings and contemporary descriptions of instruments and their use in various writings (such as biographies, festival narratives, ritual accounts, treatises on music theory, and performance technique manuals) also contribute to the documentation.

This chapter, in particular, analyzes musical instruments dating from the 6th to the 3rd centuries BCE, found in the tombs of Magna Graecia—the territory colonized by the Greeks in southern Italy—and Sicily. The focus will be on instruments whose use has persisted over the centuries in these and nearby areas, becoming part of traditional music.

8.1 Sistra

The sistrum is a metal instrument, often U-shaped, with a handle and crossed by pairs of holes through which rods pass. These rods, thinner than the holes in the frame, rattle when the instrument is shaken. The number and thickness of the rods affect the pitch and intensity of the sound produced, but the sistrum is still considered an unpitched instrument (Fig. 22).

Fig. 22 Hellenistic-era sistrum

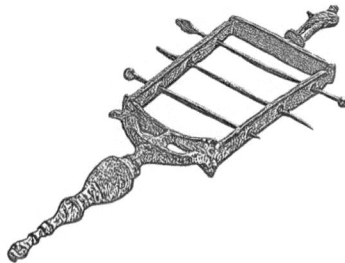

Various sources indicate that the sistrum was associated with the goddess Isis and used in rituals dedicated to her. For example, a sistrum, presumably dating to the 4th or the 3rd century BCE, found in Catania, attests to the spread of the cult of Isis in Sicily starting in the 4th century BCE (Bellia, 2012). Other sistra have been discovered in Syracuse, Herculaneum, and Pompeii.

8.2 Clappers

Clappers, specifically the type known as "with rod," consist of a central bone tablet with a handle, held in one hand, and two side plates. These plates were most likely loosely connected to the central tablet by cloth or leather strips, allowing sound production when shaken. The external plates were sometimes decorated with engravings, while the central tablet served only as a fixed element and remained undecorated (Fig. 23).

Fig. 23 Clapper with rod

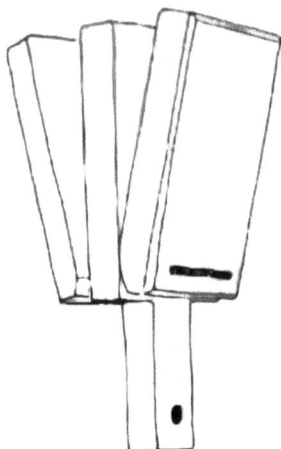

Examples have been found at Monte Sannace (near Gioia del Colle, Bari), in Taranto, and Rugge (near Lecce), inside children's tombs. Ancient literary sources also suggest that the instrument had a playful function, being suited to children's small, inexperienced hands, as well as a propitiatory function, invoking divine protection over the child (Williams, 2000). In some Taranto burials, even dolls with movable limbs holding clappers have been discovered.

Another type of clapper lacks a rod. This instrument consists of two hollow pieces made of shell, bone, ivory, metal, or wood, which are struck against each other. This type, similar to castanets, is depicted in the hands of the goddess Artemis on a 4th-century-BCE calyx crater found near Syracuse (Fig. 24).

Fig. 24 Calyx crater, 4th century BCE

Scholars believe that the image of the goddess striking the clappers, rhythmically accompanying the dance of two female figures, alludes to rites associated with the transition of girls from childhood to adulthood (Zschätzsch, 2002). Research highlights that the goddess Artemis played a significant role during puberty, a crucial stage in a woman's life at that time, presiding over the initiation of young girls into adulthood (Burkert, 1985).

8.3 Cylindrical Drums and Frame Drums (Tambourines)

Due to the decomposition of materials, no wood-and-leather drums or tambourines have been found, but their metal miniatures have been discovered. Some are metal discs with two appendages, known as "butterfly-shaped" instruments, while others have a single appendage and are referred to as "fringe-shaped" instruments (Fig. 25). Research suggests that these appendages represent the strips of cloth or leather attached to the tambourine's frame (Bellia, 2012).

Fig. 25 Miniature tambourines

Specimens of such instruments have been found in Agrigento, in the sanctuary of chthonic deities. Among these deities are Hades and Demeter, the goddess of crops and seeds, associated with rebirth after death. Scholars believe that tambourines were used in festivals celebrating the rebirth of vegetation in spring—celebrations that were widespread in Sicily and Greece (Bellia, 2012). The myth of Demeter and her daughter Persephone illustrates this concept: when Persephone was abducted by Hades, Demeter's sorrow caused the plants to stop blooming and bearing fruit. Upon Persephone's return, life resumed, marking the change of seasons.

According to a scholar, the discovery of miniature drums and tambourines in the sanctuary of chthonic deities suggests that specific music, performed with cymbals and tambourines, was used to encourage the return of the pleasant season (Zschätzsch, 2002). In general, research indicates that percussion instruments were considered particularly suitable for rituals of death and rebirth (Kolotourou, 2011), with their sounds believed to facilitate contact with deities (Bellia, 2012).

8.4 Bells, Small Bells, and Cowbells

Bells and small bells can be made from various materials, such as bronze and terracotta, and can take on shapes beyond the usual, including globular or conical forms (Fig. 26). The bells from before the Common Era that have survived are generally made of bronze, with a clapper inside the bell attached by a metal wire.

Fig. 26 Bell with a handle

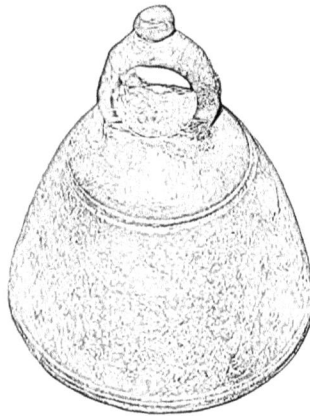

The bell likely served a summoning and signaling function in religious rites, gathering crowds. A researcher therefore presumes that its use was reserved for priests (West, 1992). Additionally, the sound of the bell was believed to ward off evil. The Latin poet Juvenal, who lived between the 1st and the 2nd centuries CE, mentions that it was customary to ring cowbells during solar or lunar eclipses to encourage a return to normalcy (Juvenal, 2011). According to a similar principle, in some Alpine villages, until a few years ago, it was customary to ring the church bell during thunderstorms to propitiate the clearing of the weather.

From a religious standpoint, certain sources, such as the writings of historian and geographer Strabo (1st century BCE–1st century CE), document a strong connection between the use of bells and Dionysian rites (Strabo, 2024). Consequently, research suggests it is likely that the bells found in the necropolis of Lilibeo-Marsala and in the sacred area of the Gela acropolis are linked to Dionysian rites (Bellia, 2012).

8.5 Auloi

A fragment of an aulos was found in Locri (Reggio Calabria), featuring three holes on the front of the pipe and one hole on the back, with Greek letters engraved near some of the holes (Fig. 27).

Fig. 27 Aulos from Locri

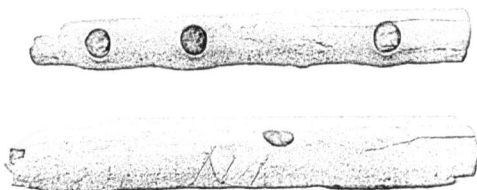

Other auloi, or aulos fragments made of bone, have been found in the sacred areas of the temples dedicated to Artemis, one in Syracuse and one in Camarina (Ragusa). The aulos found in Camarina has four holes, a flared pipe, and cross-shaped engravings (Fig. 28).

Fig. 28 Aulos from Camarina

The aulos could be single or double, the latter known as a *diaulos*. The pipes could either be of the same length, held side by side, or of different lengths, held apart. The musician operated the left pipe with the left hand and the right pipe with the right hand, each independently. Often, one of the two tubes had fewer holes than the other, allowing merely for harmonic and rhythmic counterpoints in the accompaniment.

For most Greek auloi, as well as Etruscan and Latin *tibiae*, iconographic sources suggest the use of a double reed, making the auloi similar to the modern oboe.

The Greeks and Romans had various types of double oboes: some had pipes of different lengths (like the Phrygian oboe), while others had pipes of the same length (like the Lydian double oboe, called *tibiae serranae* by the Romans, with "serranae" meaning Phoenician).

Therefore, the aulos likely had a double reed. However, research has shown that a double-pipe instrument called *auloi gamelioi* in Greek, described in ancient texts as having "two tongues," was not a single instrument with two pipes sharing a double reed but rather two pipes bound together, each with a single beating reed (Fara, 1997). Thus, it is possible that some types of auloi had a single reed. Additionally, a scholar believes that there were auloi without reeds, resembling the modern recorder (Howard, 1893).

Some auloi have been found alongside votive statuettes depicting people engaged in singing and dancing, leading a scholar to consider these instruments as integral to ceremonies and activities preparing girls for marriage (Bellia, 2009).

The aulos is described in literary sources as an instrument associated with otherworldly happiness and a symposium held in the afterlife (Colesanti, 1999; Camerotto, 2005). Historically, the symposium constituted the second part of the Greek and Roman banquet, where guests, after eating, drank wine, sang, recited poems, watched various entertainments, and conversed.

The symposium was a form of entertainment requiring significant expense for the host, as it was preceded by a banquet, wine was offered, girls were present to entertain the guests, games and musical performances were organized. This suggests it was reserved for the elite. Thus, finding one or more auloi in a tomb is considered an indicator that the deceased belonged to the aristocracy, both in the colonies of southern Italy and in mainland Greece.

Moreover, research has shown that the aulos, besides indicating the symposium in the afterlife, was the most used instrument in funeral rites, symbolizing both the deceased's entry into the afterlife, and also the community coming together around the family and friends of the deceased, in order to offer emotional support and comfort (Johnston, 1999).

Furthermore, a scholar has noted that in Syracuse, during the festival honoring Artemis, protector of childbirth and facilitator of labor and birth, a dance accompanied by the aulos was performed (Albertocchi, 2018).

A bas-relief on a funerary stele from the 6th to the 5th century BCE, preserved in the Antonino Salinas Regional Archaeological Museum in Palermo, shows an aulos player wearing a characteristic "muzzle" called *phorbeia*, which helped maintain the correct positioning and use of the instrument.

8.6 Conch Shell Trumpets

Musicologist Giulio Fara, active in the early 1900s, hypothesized that in ancient times, people found large shells on the seashore and removed the mollusk inside for consumption. To eat the remaining bits of the mollusk, they likely broke the shell's tip and then blew into the shell while pressing their lips together, with their lips acting as reeds and causing the shell's inner air to vibrate, producing a deep sound (Fara, 1997). This sound was used for signaling, gathering people and flocks, and later as a signal for attack and war.

The conch shell trumpet can produce only one or two tones, limiting its use to signaling and calling. It was also believed to ward off evil and was used to mark the beginning of various sacred ceremonies. Scholars suggest that the marine origin of the instrument may be connected to the protection of cliffs and activities related to navigation and fishing. Additionally, conch shell trumpets were sometimes placed in building foundations, likely to place the structures being built under the protection of marine deities (Bellia, 2012).

In Locri (Reggio Calabria), a conch shell trumpet, dated from the 6th to the 4th centuries BCE, was found. The instrument has a hole at the apex for blowing and two finger holes. Other conch shell trumpets from the 3rd century BCE have been discovered in the necropolises of Heraclea (a location today called Policoro, in Basilicata) and Morgantina (Enna, Sicily), featuring an opening at the apex for blowing but without finger holes.

Summary

The second part of this book, titled *Analogies Between Archaeological Finds and Contemporary Instruments*, encompasses Chapters 8 and 9. It begins by exploring the concept of culture. In a narrow sense, culture refers to the intellectual development of an individual, including knowledge of literature, history, and the arts. However, in a broader sense, culture includes the ways in which a particular community addresses its existential challenges. Once effective solutions to fundamental problems (such as securing food, building shelters, and maintaining social order) are established, they are passed down through generations. In fact, although a community's needs may evolve over time, some remain constant despite the passage of time.

Music and musical instruments play an integral role in a group's culture. Evidence of ancient musical practices can be found in the instruments themselves, in depictions such as vase paintings, and in written descriptions from various sources, including biographies, festival and ritual accounts, as well as treatises on music theory and performance techniques. This chapter examines musical instruments dating from the 6th to the 3rd centuries BCE, discovered in Magna Graecia and Sicily, including sistra, clappers, drums, tambourines, bells, auloi, and conch shell trumpets.

Keywords

Auloi, *Auloi Gamelioi*, Clappers, Conch Shell Trumpets, Cylindrical Drums and Frame Drums (Tambourines), Everyday Objects, Funeral Ceremonies, Narratives of Festivals and Various Rituals, Sistra, *Tibiae Serranae*, Treatises on Musical Theory, Vase Paintings.

Preeminent Figures

- Artemis
- Demeter, Persephone, and Hades
- Isis

Questions for Review

1. What is meant by *culture*?
2. What are the main factors that influence a community's strategies for addressing its fundamental problems?
3. Within a community, are there needs that evolve over time and others that remain constant?
4. What is the relationship between a group's religion and its culture?
5. What are the primary sources that document ancient musical practices?
6. Do we possess archaeological artifacts of sistra, clappers, drums, tambourines, bells, small bells, auloi, and conch shell trumpets?
7. Where have archaeological artifacts of various instruments been found?
8. Which instruments were considered particularly suitable for death and rebirth rituals?

Further Reading and Online Resources

Albertocchi, Marina. "Osservazioni in merito alla rappresentazione della gravidanza nella coroplastica greca." In *Simbolo e gesto. La determinazione di genere nelle statuette fittili del mondo greco, Quaderni di Archeologia*, edited by Marina Albertocchi, Nicola Cucuzza, Bianca Maria Giannattasio, 57–74. Genova, Italy/2, Roma: Aracne Editrice, 2018.

Bartoccini, Renato. "Taranto: Rinvenimenti e scavi (1933–34)." *Notizie e scavi*, s.VI, XII, 1936: 107–232.

Bellia, Angela. *Coroplastica con raffigurazioni musicali nella Sicilia greca (VI–III sec. a.C.)*. Pisa-Roma, Italy: Fabrizio Serra, 2009.

Bellia, Angela. "Le raffigurazioni musicali nei Cippi funerari della Collezione Casuccini del Museo Archeologico Regionale 'A. Salinas' di Palermo." In *La musica in Etruria*, edited by M. Carrese, E. Licastro, M. Martinelli, 59–66. Tarquinia, Italy: Comune di Tarquinia, 2010.

Bellia, Angela. *Strumenti musicali e oggetti sonori nell'Italia meridionale e in Sicilia (VI–III sec. a.C.). Funzioni rituali e contesti*. Lucca, Italy: LIM, 2012.

Burkert, Walter. *Greek Religion, in the Archaic and Classical Periods*. Hoboken, NJ: Blackwell, 1985.

Camerotto, Alberto. "Voci e suoni dall'aldilà. L'utopia musicale dell'Elisio in Luciano di Samosata (VH II 5–16)." *Musica e storia*, XIII, 1, 2005: 101–129.

Colesanti, Giulio. "Il simposio in Omero." *Materiali e discussioni*, XLIII, 1999: 41–76.

Fara, Giulio. *Sulla musica popolare in Sardegna*, edited by Gian Nicola Spanu. Nuoro, Italy: Ilisso, 1997.

Howard, Albert A. "The Αὐλός or Tibia." *Harvard Studies in Classical Philology*, 4, 1893: 1–60.

Johnston, Sarah Iles. *Restless Dead. Encounters Between the Living and the Dead in Ancient Greece*. Berkeley-Los Angeles-London: University of California, 1999.

Juvenal. "The Satires." Translated by A. S. Kline, *Poetry in Translation*, 2011. Accessed November 3, 2024. https://www.poetryintranslation.com/.

Kolotourou, Katerina. "Musical Rhythms from the Cradle to the Grave." In *Current Approaches to Religion in Ancient Greece: Papers Presented at a Symposium at the Swedish Institute (Athens, April 17–19, 2008)*, edited by Matthew Haysom and Jenny Wallensten, 169–187. Stockholm: Skrifta Utgivna av Svenska Institutet, 2011.

Lopinto, Linda. *La musica degli dei: gli strumenti musicali nell'iconografia di Apollo sulla ceramica italiota*. Fasano, Italy: Schena, 1995.

Roy, Olivier. *Holy Ignorance: When Religion and Culture Part Ways*. New York: Columbia University Press, 2010.

Strabo. *Strabo's Geography: A Translation for the Modern World*. Translated by Sarah Pothecary. Princeton, NJ: Princeton University Press, 2024.

West, Martin Litchfield. *Ancient Greek Music*. Oxford: Oxford University Press, 1992.

Williams, Dyfri. "Of Geometric Toys, Symbols and Votives." In *Periplous: Papers on Classical Art and Archaeology Presented to Sir John Boardman*, edited by G. R. Tsetskhladze, A. J. N. W. Prag, and A. M. Snodgrass, 39192. London: Thames & Hudson, 2000.

Zschätzsch, Anemone. *Verwendung und Bedeutung griechischer Musikinstrumente in Mythos und Kult*. Rahden, Germany: Marie Leidorf, 2002.

CHAPTER 9

Instruments Still Used Today in Traditional Music

After describing the characteristics, uses, and functions of some instruments from before the Common Era, it is time to determine which of these instruments are still used in traditional and folk music, or were at least in use until the second half of the 19th century.

9.1 Sistra, Clappers, and Tambourines

In the book *Dei costumi dell'isola di Sardegna* [On the Customs of the Island of Sardinia], scholar Antonio Bresciani (1850) mentions that sistra, clappers, and tambourines were still in use in Sardinia. Specifically, the author notes the use of sistra during wedding ceremonies; along with other instruments, they announced the arrival of the bride and groom, to whom all the women of the village would throw handfuls of grain, wishing them good fortune. During the wedding banquet, young girls played the clappers and sang wedding hymns, while verses were improvised about the families of the bride and groom. The celebration ended with dancing.

9.2 Bells and Cowbells

Bells are part of the struck idiophones sub-class, where the instrument is struck by a nonresonant device. In the case of bells, the nonresonant device is the clapper or striker of the bell. Some types of bells still in use today in Sardinia employ a different sound mechanism compared to those in most of Italy. In most of Italy, the bell swings, while in Sardinia, the bell remains mostly stationary, with one or more ropes being pulled to move the clapper(s) (Fig. 29). This method allows the bell ringer to create rapid and lively rhythms, as well as rather complex patterns.

When bells were operated manually, the bell ringer typically had two to four bells of different pitches at their disposal and had to skillfully combine the tolls according to initial formulas and final cadences.

Fig. 29 Belltower of the Church of St. Leonard, Masullas

Bells are used to send sound signals that mark the time of day: in Sardinian popular devotions, such as in the Liturgy of the Hours, prayers are recited at specific times following the call of the bell—at dawn, noon, and evening. Different bell patterns marked other occasions: festive bells, passing bells, death knells, Mass, and a particularly solemn ringing for Easter Mass.

Everyone knew how to interpret the bell signals, and poems—both serious and humorous ones—were often composed to the melody of the different tolls. Besides their sacred use, bells also had secular applications, such as the tocsin, which signaled a fire alarm and called all the men to gather and extinguish it.

Cowbells, known as *sonazzos*, are similar to bells and are usually tied around the necks of animals in herds to signal their presence and prevent them from straying. On some occasions, however, they are used by humans as actual musical instruments.

There are different types, used in various areas: round-shaped *sonazzos* (used in the Campidano region), elongated and narrow-shaped ones (used in Narbolia), and square-shaped ones (used in northern Sardinia) (Fig. 30).

Fig. 30 Sonazzos

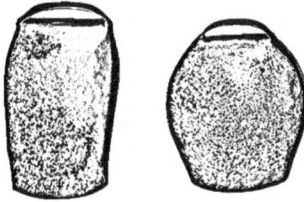

During Carnival in some towns in Sardinia, certain figures, known as *mamuthones* in Mamoiada, wear sleeveless overcoats made of black sheep skins and frightening masks, alluding to the wild and demonic. These figures are equipped with cowbells. In the case of the *mamuthones*, the *sonazzos* are attached to leather harnesses and hang from the shoulders and chest. The *mamuthones* walk slowly and make sudden movements of their torsos, setting the *sonazzos* in motion. In these *sonazzos* used by the *mamuthones*, the sound is produced both by the clappers of the cowbells and by the impact of the various cowbells striking against each other (Fig. 31).

Fig. 31 Mamuthone

There are also other forms of costuming similar to that used by the *mamuthones*, which have equally ancient origins and are still in use among some peoples of Thrace and the Eastern Mediterranean. Comparable to the *mamuthones* are the *thurpos* from Orotelli (Nuoro), figures who wear a dark coat. They do not use masks to conceal their faces, which are simply blackened with soot, and they mimic the yoke of oxen engaged in plowing (Fig. 32).

Fig. 32 Thurpos

Ethnomusicologist Sergio Bonanzinga attests to the use of bells for purely musical purposes in Sicily during the Christmas period. In the Mother Church of Isnello, Sicily, a unique tradition comes to life on Christmas Eve. Five bells are played by two individuals using large hemp ropes: the most experienced bell ringer, usually the sacristan, plays three bells simultaneously. The performance lasts about 10 minutes and is based on a specific rhythmic pattern repeated several times. Bonanzinga highlights that the sound of the bells is intended to represent the ringing of the livestock that, along with the shepherds, came to watch over the baby Jesus (Bonanzinga, 2013). Scholar Maria Grazia Magazzù also notes the musical use of bells in the cult of the Annunziata in Fiumedinisi (Messina) (Magazzù, 2007).

In Sicily, some cowbells, known as *campani*, are made of bronzed sheet metal, while other types, such as *muligna* and *mulignedda*, are made from an alloy of copper, zinc, and tin. Small bells are traditionally used for apotropaic and protective purposes and are often made of silver. It is not by chance that these bells often bear the names of saints invoked for special protection, such as *campaneddu i san Giuvanni* and *campanedda i santa Barbara*.

9.3 Auloi

During the 1990s, scholar Gian Nicola Spanu attested to the continued presence of the double aulos in Sardinia (Spanu, 1994).

Ethnomusicologist Mario Sarica states that among the double-pipe instruments still being built and used in 1990 in Mili San Pietro (Messina), is the double clarinet, known as *zammare*. This instrument consists of two diverging pipes of different lengths, each fitted with a single reed. The ends of the two pipes, with the reeds, are held simultaneously in the performer's mouth. The shorter pipe, which has four front holes and one back hole, plays the melody, while the longer pipe, featuring three holes, performs a harmonic-rhythmic function (Sarica, 2004).

Scholars note that, while it is not possible to determine whether this instrument directly descended from the aulos, it is likely that its distant ancestors can be identified among reed instruments, whose descendants include the aulos and the Roman *tibia* (Baines, 1961). According to this theory, it is possible to identify an "organological kinship" between the double clarinet and the aulos, due to a shared distant ancestor.

9.4 Conch Shell Trumpets

Among the folk instruments of Sicily is the conch shell trumpet, called *brogna* or *trumma*, generally considered a simple sound object used for signaling purposes—for example, in oil mills and grain mills. However, the *brogna* also plays a purely musical role in various festive contexts. In a conch shell trumpet from the early 20th century, preserved in the Museum of Popular Culture and Music of the Peloritani in Messina, two holes can be identified: the blowing hole, created by cutting the apex of the shell, and another hole, whose function is not to modulate the sound but rather to allow a cord to pass through (Fig. 33). By means of this cord, the instrument was hung on the walls of the places where it was customarily used, such as oil mills and grain mills.

Fig. 33 Conch shell trumpet

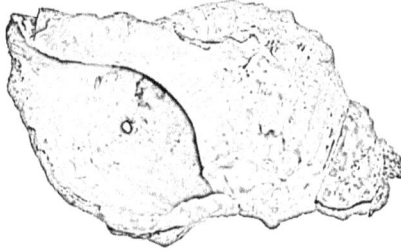

In Sardinia, the conch shell trumpet, called *corru marinu*, was played, along with the percussion of stones, old boilers, and the dragging of chains, to perform a "mock serenade" intended to humorously celebrate the second marriage of a widower or a widow (Calvia, 1894; Gioielli, 2005).

9.5 Concluding Reflections

At the current stage of research, it is not known for certain whether there is a direct connection between ancient instruments from before the Common Era and those used in the traditional and folk music of southern Italy. Some scholars, such as Pietro Sassu, believe that in Sardinia, the continuity between the use of musical instruments in ancient times and their use in oral traditional music today can be regarded as established (Sassu, 1982). In any case, we can say with certainty that the same types of instruments have been used by the same communities for very long periods.

Summary

This chapter focuses on instruments like those discussed in Chapter 8, which are still used in traditional and folk music, or at least were in use until the late 19th century. It explores their construction and functional characteristics, construction techniques, and occasions of use. The chapter also highlights that, at the current stage of research, it remains uncertain whether a direct connection always exists between ancient instruments from before the Common Era and those used in the traditional and folk music of southern Italy. However, it is clear that certain types of instruments have been used by the same communities for extended periods, and in many cases, a well-established continuity exists between the use of these instruments in ancient times and their role in oral traditional music today.

Keywords

Bells and Cowbells, *Brogna*, Clappers, *Mamuthones*, Office of the Hours, Sistra, *Sonazzos*, Tambourines, *Thurpos*, Wedding Ceremonies, *Zammare*.

Preeminent Figures

- Antonio Bresciani
- Gian Nicola Spanu
- Giuseppe Calvia
- Maria Grazia Magazzù
- Mario Sarica
- Pietro Sassu
- Sergio Bonanzinga

Questions for Review

1. In Sardinia, during which ceremonies are/were sistra, clappers, and tambourines primarily used?
2. How does the sound mechanism of Sardinian bells differ from that of bells used in most of Italy?
3. Have bells had secular uses in addition to religious ones?
4. Are figures like the *mamuthones* found in other cultures?
5. What activity do the *thurpos* mimic?
6. Did the double clarinet used in the province of Messina directly originate from the aulos?
7. Can the *brogna* also serve purely musical functions?
8. Has research established a direct connection between ancient instruments from before the Common Era and those used in traditional and folk music of southern Italy?

Further Reading and Online Resources

Baines, Anthony, ed. *Musical Instruments Through the Ages*. Harmondsworth, UK: Penguin Books, 1961.

Bonanzinga, Sergio. "Sugli strumenti musicali popolari in Sicilia." In *Strumenti musicali in Sicilia*, edited by Giovanni Paolo Di Stefano, Selima Giorgia Giuliano, and Sandra Proto, 53–90. CRicd, Palermo, Italy: Regione Siciliana, 2013.

Bresciani, Antonio. *Dei costumi dell'isola di Sardegna comparati cogli antichissimi popoli orientali*, 2 vols. Napoli, Italy: All'Uffizio della Civiltà Cattolica, 1850.

Calvia, Giuseppe. "Sas correddas." *Rivista delle tradizioni popolari italiane*, II, f. 1, 1894: 33.

Gioielli, Mauro. "La scurdia, un'antica usanza per le nozze dei vedovi." *Utriculus*, 35, July–September 2005: 4–7.

Magazzù, Maria Grazia. *Il canto della Vara e le tradizioni musicali di Fiumedinisi*, with an attached CD. Lucca, Italy: Libreria Musicale Italiana, 2007.

Sarica, Mario. *Strumenti musicali popolari in Sicilia: provincia di Messina*. Messina, Italy: Assessorato alla Cultura—Provincia Regionale di Messina, 2004.

Sassu, Pietro. "La musica di tradizione orale." In *La Sardegna: Enciclopedia*, edited by Manlio Brigaglia, II, 140–148. Cagliari, Italy: Della Torre, 1982.

Spanu, Gian Nicola. "Gli strumenti della musica popolare nell'arte sarda." In *Sonos: strumenti della musica popolare sarda*, edited by Gian Nicola Spanu, 27–33. Nuoro, Italy: ISRE Ilisso Edizioni, 1994.

PART 3

Occasions and Instruments of Oral Traditional Music

CHAPTER 10

Occasions for Making Oral Traditional Music

Chapter 3 mentioned that the field of ethno-organology studies not only musical instruments themselves but also their history and geographical diffusion. This involves examining, among other aspects, the naming of instruments, which can sometimes reveal analogies with the names of similar instruments from other cultures. For example, the *alboka*, an instrument typical of the Basque Country, derives its name from the Arabic *al-bûq* (literally "the trumpet"), an instrument likely brought to the Iberian Peninsula during the Arab occupation. The history and geographical distribution of musical instruments are closely intertwined with their description.

The second major area of study concerns the occasions on which music is made, encompassing the context in which instruments are played and the function of the performance (e.g., ritual, ceremonial, hedonistic, pedagogical, or as an accompaniment to dance).

Finally, the third major area involves other topics related to the ways of playing musical instruments: the types of performances, the relationships established between an instrument and other instruments played together, the relationship between the instrument and the performer, the relationship between the performer and the audience, and, in general, the meaning attributed to these behaviors.

When examining traditional musical instruments in a region that has experienced various dominations over the centuries, it is easy to imagine that each instrument, along with the contexts in which it is used and the meanings attributed to its use, reflects the different cultures that have existed in that territory. These cultures did not disappear with the arrival of new dominations and the cultures they brought with them but were instead partially preserved and overlapped.

An instrument "imported" from another culture undergoes processes of interference and hybridization in its new environment, significantly impacting the music played on it and the aesthetic conception to which the new music adheres.

Consider Sicily, a central meeting point in the Mediterranean that has witnessed the influence of various cultures brought by different periods of colonization and rule over the centuries. The Greek colonization occurred from the 8th to the 3rd century BCE. During the same period, the westernmost part of the island experienced Punic or Carthaginian colonization, with its most important city being what is now known as Palermo. Roman domination lasted from 241 BCE to the 5th century CE, and the most important cities of Sicily during this period were Agrigento, Catania, Trapani, Marsala, Messina, Syracuse, Taormina, and Termini Imerese. Byzantine rule extended from 535 to 553 CE, followed by Islamic rule from 827 to 1091. Norman domination spanned from 1061 to 1198, Swabian rule lasted from 1194 to 1266, Angevin domination continued from 1266 to 1282, and Aragonese rule endured from 1282 to 1516. Direct Spanish rule persisted from 1516 to 1713, followed by Savoyard rule from 1713 to 1720, Austrian control from 1720 to 1734, and finally Bourbon rule from 1735 to 1860.

Except for brief periods of domination, those that lasted several years likely brought their culture, particularly their musical culture, to Sicily. As demonstrated in Chapters 8 and 9, Sicily has preserved instruments associated with Greek colonization and others of North African origin, as attested by bibliographic sources, iconographic evidence, and travelers' accounts. These varied influences have resulted in the coexistence of traces of different cultures in Sicily, which have merged and evolved through interaction with the local culture.

The three main fields of ethno-organological research are: 1) musical instruments themselves; 2) occasions on which music is performed; and 3) types of performances. Let us begin our discussion with the last two areas, which are closely connected: the occasions for making music and the ways of performing that characterize different musical events.

Traditional occasions for making music include:

- Work songs,
- Devotional songs,
- Easter period music,
- Processions,
- Funeral laments,
- Historical reenactments,
- Storyteller performances, and
- Sardinian guitar singing.

10.1 Work Songs

In Sicily, work songs accompanied various types of work, including harvesting, threshing, grape picking, sulfur and gypsum mining, tuna fishing, salt collecting, and the transport and distribution of goods by carters and street vendors.

Sergio Bonanzinga describes the music that accompanied the transport of baskets full of grapes during the harvest. The baskets, called *còfini* (Fig. 34), made of woven wicker and reeds, weighed about 80 kg when full and had to be carried from the vineyards to the vats (*pammenti*) in the town center, where the grapes were pressed and fermented.

Fig. 34 Còfino

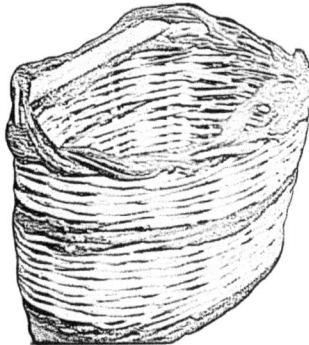

The route was long and arduous, and music and singing helped make the journey less tiring. The procession of farmers was led by a bagpiper (*ciaramid-daru*), followed by the team leader (*capu-ggiumma*), and then the other farmers carrying the *còfini*.

The music had the following structure:

- The bagpiper played a short instrumental prelude with a free rhythm.
- The song (*canzuna*) was intoned.
- The bagpiper played an instrumental interlude with a dance rhythm (*passata i bballittu*), repeated at the end of each sung stanza.
- Usually, the team leader sang the solo part, and the other carriers prolonged the last syllable of each verse in chorus.

- In the cadences, the soloist and the chorus sang the same fixed notes intoned by the bagpiper.
- Upon reaching the vat, the strongest carrier would block the entrance, preventing others from unloading. The other carriers would then start dancing a tarantella, still carrying the baskets on their shoulders, to the sound of the bagpipe and a tambourine. This dance could last up to an hour (Bonanzinga, 2013).

Another important occasion was the transport of tuna. The freshly caught tuna had to be carried from the beach to the town. It was surrounded by carnations, tied with ropes, and carried on the shoulders of two men. Their step coordination was regulated by the rhythm established by the drummer (*tammurinaru*). Alberto Favara noted that the *tammurinaru*'s role was so important that if the tuna's owner did not pay the drummer's fee, the carriers would prefer to pay it themselves. The rhythmic sound of the drum facilitated the carriers' coordination and announced the arrival of the freshly caught tuna to the town (Favara, 1923).

10.2 Devotional Songs

In Sicily, until not many years ago, celebrations according to the liturgical calendar were held not only in churches but also in the homes of the faithful. These performances could take place indoors, in front of nativity scenes or sacred images, or outdoors near a votive shrine often adorned with citrus branches full of leaves and fruits.

These domestic performances frequently occurred during novenas—cycles of prayers recited daily for 9 days, or long songs divided into 9 daily segments (*iurnati*). Hosting a novena at home often stemmed from a vow, and the family would offer food and drinks to the participants.

These rites were often officiated by wandering singers and musicians known as *orbi—blind performers referred to in various dialects as obbi, uoibbi, orvi, ovvi, uorvi, or uòrvini*—who performed religious songs composed by both laypeople and clergy. Other performers included pairs of bagpipers and singers active during the Christmas period in Palermo and Monreale. Common periods for these celebrations were:

- November 29–December 7 (novena of the Immaculate Conception)
- December 16–24 (Christmas novena)
- December 29–January 5 (octave of the Epiphany)

The repertoire included sacred stories about the life of Jesus, particularly relating to Christmas and the Passion, as well as the lives of saints, along with instrumental music such as *pasturali* (pastorales). Often, different texts were adapted to the same melody, as is common in oral traditional music.

In the Agrigento area, the Nativity is celebrated from December 26 to January 6, with songs and instrumental music related to the Nativity. In Montedoro (Caltanissetta), one of the most performed pieces is *Viaggiu dulurusu di Maria Santissima e lu patriarca S. Giuseppi in Betlemmi* [The Sorrowful Journey of the Blessed Mary and the Patriarch Saint Joseph to Bethlehem], composed around the mid-18th century by Binidittu Annuleru, a pseudonym used by a priest from Monreale, Antonino Diliberto, when publishing the poem.

10.3 Easter Period Music

Another occasion for celebrations accompanied by music is the period of Lent and Easter. In Sicily, penitential practices, ritual dramatizations, and laments were performed during the Passion. During the Easter Triduum, which spans from the evening Mass on Holy Thursday to the evening Mass on Easter Sunday, songs are performed, accompanied by clappers, drums, and trumpets.

Similarly, in some Sardinian towns the days of the Triduum were known as "the days of noise." It is important to note that during the Easter Triduum, the bells are tied and remain silent, from the *Gloria* on Holy Thursday until the *Gloria* on Easter Sunday. Since the bells cannot ring, they are replaced by wooden instruments that produce a dry, unsettling, and rather unpleasant sound, called *sonus lignorum* (sound produced by wooden instruments).

Since the bells are silent, children roam the town making noise with clappers and rattles to call the faithful to religious services. These instruments are described in Chapter 11. The noise is also produced in the church after the *Tenebrae* (Matins of Darkness), either by striking kneelers, books, confessionals, and doors or, more specifically, by shaking characteristic wooden noisemakers.

The Matins of Darkness, observed on Wednesday, Thursday, and Good Friday, is named to evoke the darkness of night, as in ancient times the office of Matins took place at night. The *Tenebrae* is a nocturnal prayer that was observed during the first three centuries of the Common Era when Christians were persecuted. For safety reasons, during these dangerous periods, Christian communities lived as secretly as possible and celebrated religious rites at times they were less likely to be detected. The Matins of Darkness is one of the most evocative rites of Holy Week in the Catholic tradition, preserved through the centuries.

Scholars believe that the custom of making noise at the end of the Matins of Darkness was widespread in large parts of France, Spain, and central and northern Italy, beginning in the Early Middle Ages (from 476 to 1000 CE), a period for which there are many testimonies of these practices, until the liturgical reforms of the Second Vatican Council (Angioni, 1994; Grassi, 1990; Ricci, 1996). This custom is evidently an apotropaic rite, meaning a rite intended to ward off evil and evil spirits, thereby protecting people, livestock, and crops.

According to ecclesiastical tradition, the loud noises in the streets and in the church during the Easter Triduum allude to the shouting of the Jews and the Roman soldiers during the Passion of Jesus, from his arrest to his crucifixion.

Similarly to a custom in Sardinia, in Calabria during the ceremonies of Tenebrae, the faithful strike, with great force, benches, confessionals, doors, or large boards specially placed on the floor of the church, to evoke the eclipse ("darkness came over the whole land," Mark 15:33) and the earthquake ("the earth shook, the rocks split," Matthew 27:51), events that, according to the Gospel, accompanied the Passion and death of Jesus (Vatican, 2002). Scholars have emphasized that the noise is meant to evoke a sense of fear and unease, reflecting the grief and despair experienced by Jesus' disciples at his death (R. Tucci, 2007).

In Calabria, certain idiophones are traditionally used only during Holy Week, from Holy Thursday to Holy Saturday, often during processions. For example, in Cassano allo Ionio (Cosenza), the Holy Thursday procession, which takes place inside the cathedral, and the Good Friday procession, which traverses the city, are accompanied by a *tràccola* (whose performer is hooded), two military drums, and a buccina, a brass instrument used in the ancient Roman army. The flagellants rhythmically beat themselves with their metal instruments, creating a unified rhythmic pattern.

Traditionally, in Calabrian towns, the idiophones of Holy Week are used exclusively by males, predominantly in the age group ranging from childhood to adolescence. Ratchets and rattles are often used during Holy Week by children and young people who roam the town to signal the time of the services. At the end of Holy Saturday, most of these instruments are stored in designated spaces in churches, confraternity headquarters, or even in wardrobes in homes. However, scholars have noted that the simpler instruments, such as the bullroarer used during Holy Week rites in some locations in the province of Catanzaro (Sant'Andrea Ionio, San Sostene, Soverato), are discarded and remade anew each year (R. Tucci, 2007; G. Tucci, 1954–1955).

10.4 Processions

In various towns in Sicily, processions in honor of St. Joseph are characterized by songs, declaimed texts, cries of invocation, rhythmic drum sequences, and band accompaniment. In Leonessa (Rieti), during processions held for the solemnity of Corpus Christi and on February 4 to celebrate the feast of the patron saint, St. Joseph of Leonessa, the bell ringers continuously ring the church bells throughout the entire procession. In Taranto, the *troccola*, a type of rattle, plays a primary role in initiating the Procession of the Mysteries, held on Good Friday, and in guiding the entire rite: it sets the pace of the procession and alternates with the music of the band.

Ratchets traditionally accompany Good Friday processions in many towns across Italy. Among those in southern Italy are Toritto (Bari), Salve (Lecce), Sorrento (Naples), San Valentino in Abruzzo Citeriore (Pescara), and Lanciano (Chieti). In these processions, the ratchets announce the appearance of Simon of Cyrene, who helped Jesus carry the cross. During the stops of the procession in Lanciano, pieces by the chapel master from Lanciano, Francesco Paolo Masciangelo (1823–1906), are performed, including the *Miserere grande* [Great Miserere] and *Christus factus est* [Christ became].

10.5 Funeral Laments

Music is also present in funeral rites and processions. Throughout the Mediterranean area, women have played a central role in funeral lamentation for centuries: both the deceased's relatives and paid professional mourners, known as *prefiche*, expressed the community's grief through melodies and gestures of despair. Among these signs of despair, the mourners often rhythmically beat their breast while singing, turning their own bodies into percussion instruments. Research has shown that funeral laments, practiced throughout southern Italy until the mid-20th century and still performed privately in Sicily, serve to formalize and symbolically reshape the grief over the loss of a loved one (Plastino, 1995; Bonanzinga, 2013).

10.6 Historical Reenactments

In Monforte San Giorgio (Messina), between January 17 and February 5, the feast of St. Agatha is celebrated, during which a true historical reenactment is performed exclusively through musical means. At dawn and dusk, the *campaniata* takes place, a series of short pieces performed from the bell tower of St. Agatha's church using two bells and a drum. The *campaniata* commemorates the liberation of Sicily from Muslim domination by the Christian army led by Roger of Hauteville, a campaign that lasted over 30 years, from 1061 to 1091. A scholar has noted that the instruments of the *campaniata*—the bells symbolizing Christianity and the drum representing the Muslim world—specifically allude to historical events and legends. Through rhythmic combinations, timbral effects, and dynamic and agogic variations, references are made to the camel's gait (which, according to tradition, was Roger's mount), the arrival of the army, the battle, and the celebratory dance of thanksgiving for the victory (Bonanzinga, 2005).

10.7 Storytellers' Performances

Storytellers were entertainers who traveled from village to village, declaiming and singing poetic texts of a popular genre. Their communication was verbal, musical, and visual, as the story narrated in each of the performed texts was painted in vivid colors on a large billboard, to which the storyteller pointed while illustrating the various moments of the tale. The stories often revolved around unrequited love, crime, miracles, and similar themes. The accompaniment was mainly provided by guitar and diatonic accordion. The figure of the storyteller has an ancient tradition in Sicily, where it flourished in the 14th century. As Angelo Clemente has pointed out, with the spread of printing, storytellers played a "journalistic" role, disseminating events and news, and selling printed leaflets containing this information to the public (Clemente, n.d.).

10.8 Sardinian Guitar Singing

A typical Sardinian tradition involving a musical instrument is *canto a chitarra* (singing with guitar accompaniment), a performance in which a larger-than-usual guitar, tuned differently, is used, typically achieving a range approximately a fourth lower than standard.

To perform *canto a chitarra*, the guitarist must first know how to accompany, on the spot, the improvisations of poet-singers, which are based on preexisting melodic models. The accompaniment alternates between two techniques: *raschiata* and *puntata*. The *raschiata* technique is similar to the Spanish *rasgueado* and involves strumming the pick or one or more fingers across some strings to produce multiple notes together or in rapid succession. In the *puntata* technique, individual notes are played, typically during virtuosic interludes between poetic stanzas.

This type of accompaniment is mostly based on major chords and can be linked to *canto a sonettu*, which is Sardinian singing accompanied by a diatonic accordion. However, it should be noted that the melodic style of the singing is archaic, giving rise to harmonic progressions that differ from classical ones.

The *canto a chitarra* is performed on occasions such as family celebrations, convivial gatherings, serenades, weddings, and in taverns. These occasions often serve to "prepare" poets and guitarists for the main events, which are singing competitions. In these competitions, performers must demonstrate their skills in 12 different forms of singing, or *boghes*, each associated with specific geographical areas, elements of traditional culture, and distinct musical characteristics. Researchers have precisely identified these distinct forms of singing:

- *Canto in re* (considered the archetype of other forms)
- *La nuoresa* (linked to funeral lamentations)
- *I mutos*
- *La galluresa*
- *La filognana* (connected to wool carding gatherings)
- *La corsicana* (the only competition form in minor mode)
- *Il trallalleru*
- *Il mi e la* (originated among the fishermen of Bosa; mi and la refer to the predominant E and A chords)
- *Il fa diesis* (again, the name refers to the predominant F-sharp chord)
- *L'isolana*
- *Il si bemolle* (the name refers to the predominant B-flat chord)
- *La disisperada* (originally a type of serenade rich in ornamentation) (Carpi, 1994; Spanu, 2008).

Competitions usually take place in village squares during local festivals honoring patron saints. The typical competition format involves three poet-singers competing, accompanied by a guitarist. The singers take turns singing stanza by stanza, striving to demonstrate their skill in varying and ornamenting the songs extemporaneously, with the goal of avoiding repetition as much as possible. The lyrics are predominantly about love.

Guitarists from the Campidano plain, between Cagliari and Oristano, also perform solo dance pieces. This happens when the poets need time to decide on the next theme for the competition. During this interval, the guitarist performs an instrumental dance.

Summary

The third part of this book, titled *Occasions and Instruments of Oral Traditional Music*, encompasses Chapters 10–15. Chapter 10 explores contexts in which oral traditional music is performed. Traditionally, music is created for various occasions, including 1) work songs; 2) devotional songs; 3) Easter period music; 4) funeral laments; 5) historical reenactments; 6) performances by storytellers; and 7) Sardinian guitar singing. The chapter analyzes various musical traditions, such as the work songs performed in Sicily during the grape harvest, the devotional songs performed by the *orbi* (blind musicians), often centered on episodes from the lives of Jesus and the saints, the music played during the Easter Triduum, known as "the days of noise," the music performed by assorted instrumental ensembles during processions, as well as the different forms of guitar singing that remain prevalent in Sardinia today.

Keywords

Campaniata, Canto a Sonettu, Days of Noise, Devotional Songs, Easter Period Music, Easter Triduum, Funeral Laments, Grape Harvest, Historical Reenactments, Matins of Darkness, Novenas, Occasions for Making Traditional Music, Processions, Sardinian Guitar Singing, Storyteller Performances, Tenebrae, Transport of Tuna, Work Songs.

Preeminent Figures

- Alberto Favara
- Angelo Clemente
- Binidittu Annuleru
- Francesco Paolo Masciangelo
- Roger of Hauteville
- Sergio Bonanzinga

Questions for Review

1. What were the major colonizations and dominations in Sicily?
2. On what occasions were work songs most commonly sung?
3. Who were the *orbi*, and what was their repertoire?
4. Why were the days of the Easter Triduum known as "the days of noise"?
5. What is the Matins of Darkness?
6. In Cassano allo Ionio, which rite do the flagellants participate in?
7. In which rites did the *prefiche* (professional mourners) play a significant role?
8. What is the *campaniata* of Monforte San Giorgio?
9. How many forms of Sardinian guitar singing are there?

Further Reading and Online Resources

Angioni, Giulio. "Le campane." In *Sonos: strumenti della musica popolare sarda*, edited by Gian Nicola Spanu, 49–50. Nuoro, Italy: ISRE Ilisso Edizioni, 1994.

Bonanzinga, Sergio. "Il tema della 'moresca' in Sicilia." In *Mori e Cristiani nelle feste e negli spettacoli popolari*, edited by Rosario Perricone, 74–103. Palermo, Italy: Edizioni Museo Pasqualino, 2005.

Bonanzinga, Sergio. "La musica di tradizione orale." In *Lingue e culture in Sicilia*, II, edited by Giovanni Ruffino, 189–246. Palermo, Italy: Centro di studi filologici e linguistici siciliani, 2013.

Carpi, Andrea. "La chitarra nella musica popolare sarda." In *SONOS: Strumenti della musica popolare sarda*, edited by Gian Nicola Spanu, 170–171. Nuoro, Italy: ISRE Ilisso Edizioni, 1994.

Clemente, Angelo. "Cuntastorie e Cantastorie." I.R.S.A.P. Agrigentum, n.d. Accessed November 3, 2024. https://www.irsap-agrigentum.it/Cuntastorie%20 e%20Cantastorie.htm.

Favara, Alberto. "Il ritmo nella vita e nell'arte popolare in Sicilia." *Rivista d'Italia*, XXVI, 1923, 79–99.

Grassi, Lorena. "I mattutini delle tenebre. un rito e i suoi significati." *Quaderni storici—Nuova serie*, 25, 74.2, August 1990: 563–586.

Plastino, Goffredo. "Etnomusicologia in Calabria." *Il Corriere Calabrese*, 1995: 7–54.

Ricci, Antonello. *Ascoltare il mondo: Antropologia dei suoni in un paese del Sud d'Italia*. Roma: Il Trovatore, 1996.

Spanu, Gian Nicola. "Strumenti e musiche con strumenti." *Il folklore d'Italia,* 3, 2008: 55–65.

Tucci, Giovanni. "Contributo allo studio del rombo." *Rivista di Etnografia*, VIII/IX, 1954–1955: 1–16.

Tucci, Roberta. " 'Gli strumenti delle tenebre:' Organologia della Settimana Santa in Calabria." In *Le forme della festa—La Settimana Santa in Calabria: studi e materiali*, edited by Francesco Faeta and Antonello Ricci, 337–353. Roma: Squilibri, 2007.

Vatican. "The New American Bible." 2002. Accessed November 3, 2024. https://www.vatican.va/archive/ENG0839/_INDEX.HTM.

CHAPTER 11

Instruments of Oral Traditional Music: Idiophones

Idiophones are instruments that produce sound through the vibration of the material they are made of, without the need for stretched membranes or strings. Among the idiophones used in traditional music in southern Italy are sistra, rattles, clappers, and ratchets.

11.1 Sistra

Sistra are shaken idiophones that produce sound when held and shaken. The sistrum is typically made from a U-shaped metal frame with a handle. The two arms of the U-shaped frame have three or four pairs of holes through which thin rods are horizontally inserted. When the instrument is shaken, the rods, being thinner than the holes, move and strike the U-shaped frame, creating a bright sound (Fig. 35). Sometimes, small metal rings are threaded onto the rods to enrich the instrument's sound.

Fig. 35 Sistrum

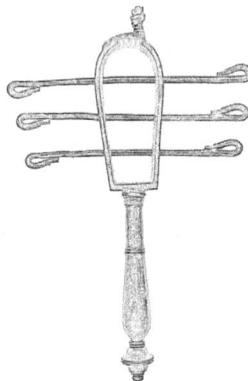

11.1.1 Abruzzese Mascrille

In Abruzzo, the *mascrille* is a specific type of sistrum known as a "half sistrum" due to its shape. Researcher Giuseppina Giovannelli notes that a curved elm branch is used in constructing a *mascrille*, to which tin jingles are attached (Fig. 36). The *mascrille* is played by shaking it or, in dance contexts, by striking it against the dancer's forearm (Giovannelli, 1988). Several specimens are preserved in the Museum of Folk Traditions in Cerqueto, near Fano Adriano (Teramo).

Fig. 36 Mascrille

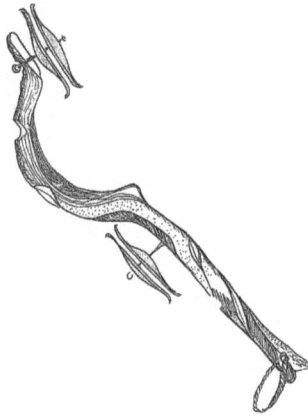

11.2 Rattles

Rattles are also shaken idiophones, where sound is produced by the performer's movements rather than by directly striking the instrument. A rattle typically consists of a wooden board or frame with one or more mobile elements—typically iron or wooden levers—hinged or mounted on the structure. When the instrument is held and shaken, either by rotating it along its longitudinal axis or by other means, the mobile components strike against the board or frame, producing a sharp and rhythmic percussive sound.

11.2.1 Abruzzese Spadaccine

The *spadaccine* from the Vestine area (a territory located in the central part of Abruzzo) is a rattle with a sharp, sword-like timbre, made from beechwood (Fig. 37). It is used during Holy Week rites.

Fig. 37 Spadaccine

11.2.2 Sardinian Matracca

In Sardinia, a type of rattle called *matracca, matràccola,* or *stròcculas* is rein-forced with strips of sheet metal and large nails at the points where the iron levers strike the wooden board (Fig. 38).

Fig. 38 Matracca

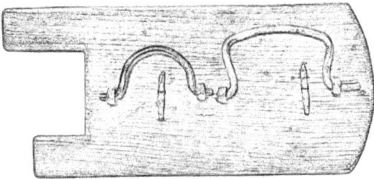

11.2.3 Sicilian Tròccula

The Sicilian *tròccula* is a rattle made from elm wood, traditionally played in the days leading up to Easter (Fig. 39): it is used on Holy Thursday to accompany the performance of the Passion songs, and on Good Friday to announce the passage of the procession.

Fig. 39 Tròccula

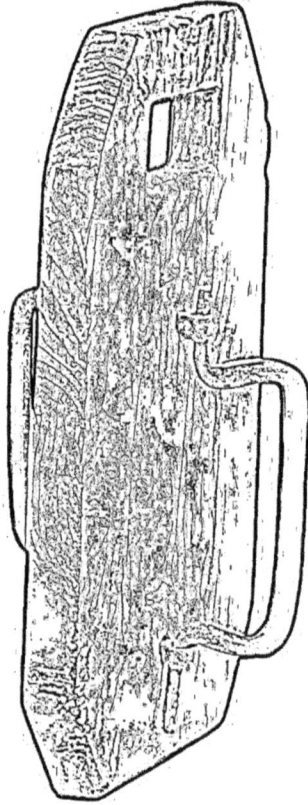

11.3 Clappers

Clappers are concussion idiophones, meaning they are instruments in which elements strike against each other to produce sound.

11.3.1 Abruzzese Valichira and Mattiaminde

In the Vestine area, instruments known as *valichira* and *mattiaminde* are types of clappers. The *valichira* is a hand-cranked clapper that produces sound when two wooden hammers, vaguely human in shape, alternately strike a slat that acts as a resonator. The instrument is mostly made from elm wood (Fig. 40), and a specimen is housed in the Museum of Folk Traditions in Cerqueto (Teramo).

Fig. 40 Valichira

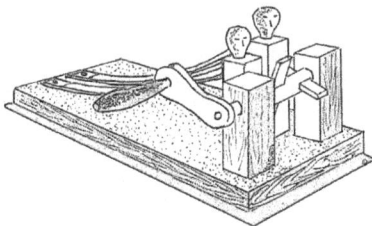

The *mattiaminde*, also known as *tippe-tappe* or *trionfe*, is similar to the Neapolitan *triccheballacche*, although the latter has three elements, with the central one being fixed. The *mattiaminde* has only two movable, scissor-like elements. Its structure is made from spruce wood, and the jingles are made of tin (Fig. 41).

Fig. 41 Mattiaminde

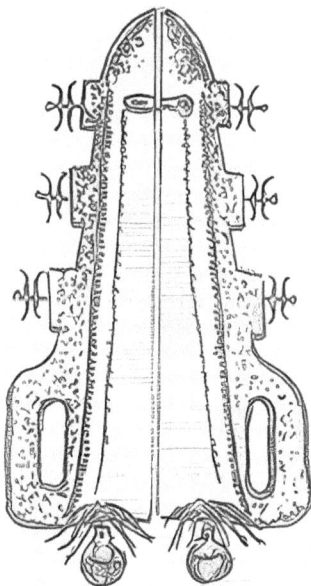

11.3.2 Sardinian Taulittas

The Sardinian idiophone known as *taulittas* also belongs to the clappers group. The *taulittas* consist of three rectangular wooden tablets joined together by a soft binding: the central tablet is larger and has a handle. When the performer shakes the instrument, the outer tablets alternately strike the central tablet (Fig. 42). *Taulittas* are used during the Easter Triduum as a substitute for the bells, which are traditionally bound and silent during that period.

Fig. 42 Taulittas

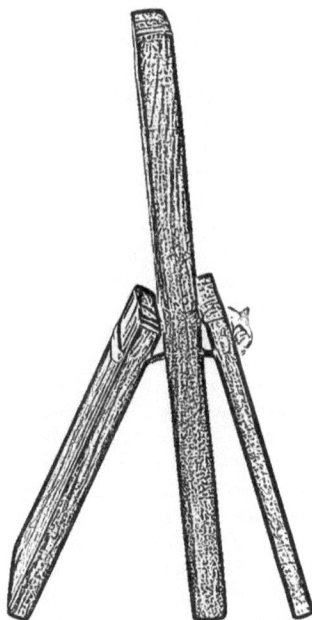

11.4 Ratchets

A ratchet is a scraped idiophone consisting of a toothed wheel fixed to a handle and mounted on a frame, with a wooden strip attached to the frame. When the instrument is held by the handle and rotated around its axis, the wooden strip scrapes against the teeth of the wheel, producing sound (Fig. 43).

Fig. 43 Ratchet

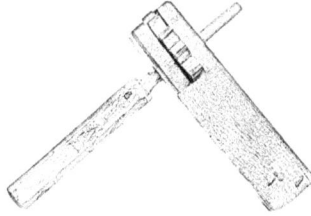

11.4.1 Abruzzese Crillone

The *crillone* from the Vestine area is a ratchet with three reeds, enclosed in a wooden box (Fig. 44). The structure is made from walnut wood, while the reeds are made from beechwood. A specimen is kept in the Church of St. Clare in Penne. The *crillone* is one of the instruments used in the rites held during the days leading up to Easter.

Fig. 44 Crillone

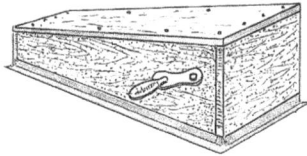

11.4.2 Sardinian Rana 'e Canna and Rana 'e Taula

In Sardinia, there are two main types of ratchets: *rana 'e canna* (also called *zaccarredda*), made from common reed (Fig. 45), and *rana 'e taula*, made from various woods. The wheel is typically made of walnut or oak, while the handle is made of strawberry tree wood (Fig. 46). These ratchets are primarily used to produce the distinctive noise associated with Holy Week.

Fig. 45 Rana 'e canna

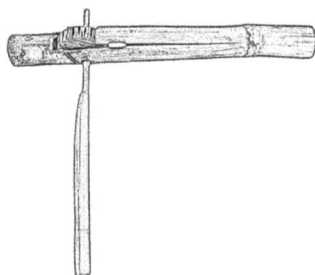

Fig. 46 Rana 'e taula

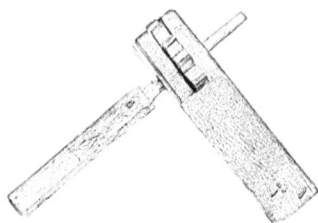

11.4.3 Salento's Trènula

Likewise, the *trènula* (also called *trozzula*) is used during Lent in Salento, a peninsula of Apulia often described as the heel of Italy's boot. When the instrument is given a circular motion, its movable part rotates, producing a dry and continuous sound. Beyond its religious use during the Easter period, the *trènula* also served as a noisemaker toy, traditionally bought during the ancient *Te lu Panieri* fair, which was enhanced in 1442 by Giovanni Antonio Orsini del Balzo, Prince of Taranto, who extended its duration to three days (Shaw Briggs, 1911).

11.5 Jaw Harp

There is some debate among scholars about how to classify the jaw harp. Erich von Hornbostel and Curt Sachs classify it as a plucked idiophone (von Hornbostel and Sachs, 1961), Ottavio Tiby includes it among percussion instruments with indefinite pitch (Tiby, 1957: I), while Sergio Bonanzinga places it in a mixed category between idiophones and aerophones (Bonanzinga, 2013).

The *scacciapensieri* (jaw harp) consists of an iron or copper wire frame, usually shaped like an onion, with a thin steel tongue fixed at its center. The metal wire frame tapers at both ends, running parallel to the steel tongue. This design allows the performer to hold the frame against their teeth, support the rounded part with one hand, and use the other hand to operate the terminal portion of the steel tongue, which extends outward at a right angle (Fig. 47).

Fig. 47 Jaw harp

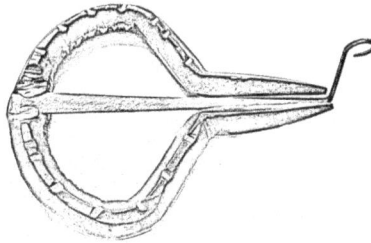

The free end of the instrument's tongue often has a curl or small ring, sometimes holding small balls of wax, which weigh down the tongue. The instrument's tuning depends on the thickness and weight of the tongue, and placing wax balls on it slightly alters its fundamental frequency. While the fundamental frequency remains fixed during the performance, serving as a drone, various harmonics can be emphasized by changing the shape of the performer's oral cavity and adjusting the position of their tongue. Rhythms, melodies, and dynamic variations are achieved by combining the rhythmic impulse from plucking the instrument's tongue with the different pitches and timbres generated by altering the shape of the oral cavity and adjusting the intensity of sounds produced by inhaling and exhaling through the mouth.

A scholar believes that the jaw harp, originally from Asia, likely arrived in the region south of the Alps from the north, through areas of continental Europe where it was initially widespread (Guizzi, 2020). However, it is also possible that it was brought to the southern regions via the Mediterranean, perhaps by the Roma people (Guizzi, 2020). This theory is supported by the name used for the instrument in Campania, *tromma de li zingari*, meaning "trumpet of the gypsies" (Sitillo, 1888). The name refers to the fact that jaw harps were traditionally made by Roma blacksmiths, who specialized in producing metal objects like boilers and other containers, which were then sold by itinerant vendors.

Other regional names include *trumbon* in Apulia, *marranzanu, nganna-lar-runi*, and *mariolu* in Sicily, and *sa trunfa* in Sardinia. While today the use of the jaw harp is documented only in certain southern regions, it was widespread in northern Italy until the early 20th century, particularly in Piedmont, where industrial production of these instruments was thriving.

In Sardinia, the jaw harp is used to accompany marches and dances. The jaw harp was once prominent in both solo and accompaniment roles; today, it is mainly played by groups involved in the folk revival.

Summary

Chapter 11 introduces a series of four chapters, each dedicated to one of the four instrument classes. This chapter focuses on idiophones, providing a detailed overview of instruments from the following groupings: 1) sistra, 2) rattles, 3) clappers, 4) ratchets, and 5) jaw harps. For the last grouping, the chapter notes that scholars are divided: some classify the jaw harp as a plucked idiophone, others consider it a percussion instrument with indeterminate pitch, while still others place it in an overlap between idiophones and aerophones. For each instrument discussed, the chapter provides its Italian name, regional dialect variations, and the traditional contexts in which it is or has been played.

Keywords

Clappers, *Crillone*, Jaw Harp, *Mascrille, Matracca, Mattiaminde, Rana 'e Canna, Rana 'e Taula*, Ratchets, Rattles, Sistra, *Spadaccine, Taulittas, Te lu Panieri, Trènula, Tròccula, Trozzula, Valichira*.

Preeminent Figures

- Curt Sachs
- Erich von Hornbostel
- Fabio Guizzi
- Giovanni Antonio Orsini del Balzo
- Giuseppina Giovannelli

- Ottavio Tiby
- Sergio Bonanzinga

Questions for Review

1. What are idiophones?
2. How is the sound of sistra and rattles produced?
3. Why is the Abruzzese *mascrille* described by researchers as a "half sistrum"?
4. How is the sound of clappers produced?
5. Why is the ratchet classified as a scraped idiophone?
6. What are the distinguishing features of the Abruzzese *crillone*?
7. What toy instrument was typically purchased for children at the *Te lu Panieri* fair?
8. What theories have been proposed regarding the arrival of the jaw harp (*scacciapensieri*) in Italy?
9. Why can the jaw harp be considered a complete musical instrument?

Further Reading and Online Resources

Bonanzinga, Sergio. "Sugli strumenti musicali popolari in Sicilia." In *Strumenti musicali in Sicilia*, edited by Giovanni Paolo Di Stefano, Selima Giorgia Giuliano, and Sandra Proto, 53–90. CRicd, Palermo, Italy: Regione Siciliana, 2013.

Giovannelli, Giuseppina. *Strumenti musicali popolari dell'area vestina.* Pescara, Italy: Editrice Italica, 1988.

Guizzi, Fabio. *Guida alla musica popolare in Italia.* Lucca, Italy: LIM, 2020.

Shaw Briggs, Martin. *In the Heel of Italy: A Study of an Unknown City.* New York: Duffield, 1911.

Sitillo, Giancola. *Nuovo dizionario napolitano—italiano compilato sulla scorta delle opere in dialetto di Giancola Sitillo: contenente in appendice un dizionarietto ortografico della lingua italiana ossia una raccolta di tutte le voci di dubbia scrittura ed anche di difficile significato ricavato dai più classici autori pel professore Antonio Greco.* Napoli, Italy: Giuseppe Eschena Libraio Editore, 1888.

Tiby, Ottavio. "Il canto popolare siciliano. Studio introduttivo," in Alberto Favara, *Corpus di musiche popolari siciliane*, 2 vols., edited by Ottavio Tiby, I, 22–113. Palermo, Italy: Accademia di Scienze Lettere e Arti di Palermo, 1957.

von Hornbostel, Erich M., and Curt Sachs. "Classification of Musical Instruments." Translated from the Original German by Anthony Baines and Klaus P. Wachsmann, *The Galpin Society Journal*, 14 (Mar.), 1961: 3–29.

CHAPTER 12

Membranophones

Membranophones are instruments that produce sound through the vibration of a stretched membrane. Within this class, two significant sub-classes can be highlighted: struck drums and friction drums. Struck drums include cylindrical drums and frame drums, or tambourines.

12.1 Cylindrical Drums

Cylindrical drums are membranophones characterized by a drum shell whose height is greater than the radius of the membrane; the drum's diameter remains consistent across its entire length, from the center to the ends. These drums can be either single-headed or double-headed.

12.1.1 Sicilian Tabbala

The *tabbala* preserved in the Museum of Culture and Popular Music of the Peloritani in Messina is a double-headed cylindrical drum. It features a wooden shell with two goat skin membranes, which are glued to the rims and secured with cords. The membrane tension is maintained by rope tensioners arranged in a Y-shape, with the Y arms connected by thin strips of leather that help maintain the tension. The instrument includes a leather strap for shoulder support and two beechwood sticks (Fig. 48).

Fig. 48 Tabbala

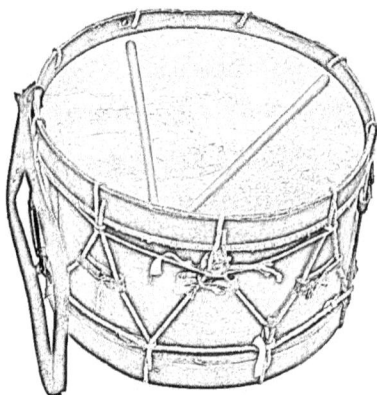

12.1.2 Sicilian Tammurinu

Also preserved in the Museum of Culture and Popular Music of the Peloritani, this cylindrical drum is worn in a bandolier style. It has a brass-plated copper shell with a diameter of about 60 cm and a height of 40 cm. Despite its name—a diminutive of *tammuru* (drum)—implying a smaller size, the drum produces a deep sound. The goat skin membranes are tensioned using Y-shaped cord tensioners, with thin leather strips binding the arms of the Y, helping to maintain the tension of the stay rods. The drum has a leather strap for shoulder support and is played with two wooden sticks (Fig. 49).

Fig. 49 Tammurinu

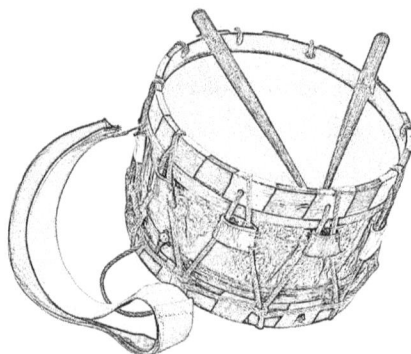

12.1.3 Tamburu from Sassari

The *tamburu* from the Sassari area, also known as the "Spanish drum," is a military drum—a double-headed cylindrical drum played while hung at the performer's side. The cylindrical shell is made of 1 mm-thick brass sheet.

The skin is tanned using the following method: first, it is immersed in quick-lime to remove the hair, and then, once mounted on a frame, it is dried in the sun. This method is also used in Campania for tanning the membrane of the *tammorra* and in Sicily for tanning the membranes of the *tammurinu*. The hoops and counterhoops are made of beechwood, with nylon cord tensioners passing through holes in the counterhoops, tightened with thin leather strips forming a Y-shape. The mallets are made of Volga pine or beechwood (Fig. 50). The Sassari *tamburu* is played in a duet with a piccolo (*pìffaru*) during the solemn mid-August procession, providing rhythm for the worshippers carrying giant candlesticks.

Fig. 50 Tamburu from Sassari

12.1.4 Tumbarinos from Gavoi

Gavoi (Nuoro) is known for its rich tradition of membranophones. Among them, this study will focus on two types in particular: the *tumbarinu* and the *tumbarinu 'e gardone*. The *tumbarinu* has a slender cylindrical shell made of beech or oak wood, about 20 cm in height and 35–40 cm in diameter. It is a double-headed drum, often made with goat skins for the membranes, though sheep, donkey, cat, or dog skins are also sometimes used. The skins are sewn onto a metal wire hoop, with tensioners inserted into holes in the skin (Fig. 51).

Fig. 51 Tumbarinu from Gavoi

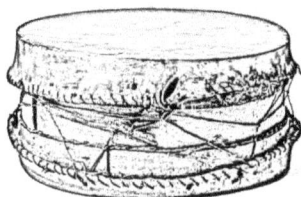

The *tumbarinu 'e gardone* features a shell made from first-cut cork, known as *gardone*. The cork is harvested in one piece, naturally suited to form the cylindrical shape required for constructing the body of the *tumbarinu*. The internal pores of the cork are sealed with glue, and the ends are joined longitudinally with iron wire or a flexible willow twig to form the cylinder. The edges are smoothed to facilitate membrane vibration.

In both types of *tumbarinu*, a cord (*bordoniera*) placed diametrically across the non-struck membrane divides it into two parts, allowing one part to vibrate sympathetically when the other membrane is struck, thereby producing the immediately higher harmonic. The mallets are made of beech, pomegranate, or chestnut wood, shaped using a knife.

In contrast to the *tamburu* from Sassari, the skins of the *tumbarinos* from Gavoi are tanned by applying a mixture of ash and hot water to the hairy side, then rolling the skin up and burying it for about ten days. Afterward, the skin is unearthed, cleaned easily, rinsed, dried, and applied to the shell. The *tumbarinos* from Gavoi serve both a ritual function, as seen in the rhythmic performances by young people in the streets during Carnival, and a more hedonistic function in multi-instrumental ensembles, which also include *pipaiolu*, *triangulu*, and *organettu*.

12.1.5 Tumbarinu from Aidomaggiore

The *tumbarinu* from Aidomaggiore (Oristano) is a double-headed drum with a cylindrical shell, originally made of cork or wood but now often made of tin. The membranes, made of dog skin, are sewn onto wooden hoops of hackberry wood. There are no counterhoops. A single cord forms the tensioners, tightened with thin leather strips in a Y-shape. The *bordoniera* is made of horsehair (Fig. 52).

Fig. 52 Tumbarinu from Aidomaggiore

The performer holds the drum with their left forearm inside a leather strap, striking the membrane with a mallet in their right hand, while the left hand uses a differently shaped mallet to dampen vibrations. By using the two mallets together, the performer creates the distinctive rhythmic sequences of the *sa cointrotza* dance, performed during Carnival by a trio consisting of *tumbarinu*, *organettu*, and *triangulu*.

12.1.6 Sardinian Tumbarineddu

This instrument is attested in the middle valley of the Tirso River. It is one of the smallest cylindrical drums, made from a knot-free cane about 12 cm in height and 5 cm in diameter. A membrane made from a bull's bladder is attached to one end and secured with several turns of string coated with tar (Fig. 53).

The membrane is played by striking it with the index and middle fingertips, while the other hand regulates sound intensity by opening and closing the open end of the pipe. The *tumbarineddu* is used to accompany dances.

Fig. 53 Sardinian Tumbarineddu

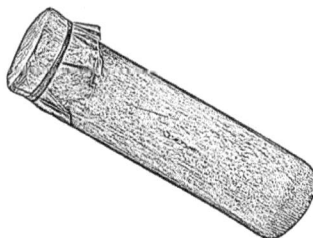

12.1.7 Abruzzese Drum

Evidence of this instrument is found in the Vestine area; the drum has a beechwood shell, approximately 41 cm in diameter and over 43 cm in height. The membranes are made of donkey skin, with hemp tensioners held in place by leather strips. The drum includes a leather strap and beechwood sticks.

12.1.8 Occasions for Drum Use

Drums are used on various occasions, such as the *Tubbiana*, held in Palermo. A scholar notes that *Tubbiana* refers not only to dance music but also to a masquerade featuring traditional figures like the Englishman, the Spaniard, the dentist, the doctor, and the architect, who dance and jump in a disorderly fashion (Pitrè, 1913). The masquerade is accompanied by a roving band consisting of *tammurinu*, *piffero*, and castanets.

In Abruzzo, the village of Pretara (Teramo) has a traditional musical group called *Li Tamurrë di Pretara*, which includes *piffero* and drums, and since 1925, also cymbals. A scholar believes the group's origins may date back to a military detachment stationed in Isola del Gran Sasso (Teramo) in 1569, which gradually began performing at civilian and religious events, such as processions (Di Silvestre, 1998, 2004). The repertoire has been maintained to this day and enriched with melodies from a popular song genre. An important performance opportunity for *Li Tamurrë di Pretara* is during the feast of St. Mary of Pagliara, celebrated on the first Sunday after Easter, in the church located on a ridge 5 km from the village. On Saturday afternoon, the music called *La Vigilia* (The Vigil) is performed. On Sunday, *La Diana* (likely referring to the morning star) is played by a fife, a drum, and a bass drum, without singing; during the procession, *La Processione* (The Procession) is performed. When the statue of the saint is returned to the church at the end of the procession, *La Casa Patrona* (The Patron's House) is played, inviting the faithful to lunch. Finally, the feast ends in the evening with Mass, during which *Il Vespro* (The Vespers) is played, again with a fife, a drum, and a bass drum.

The music generally consists of short melodies of a few measures, with repetitions characterized by grace notes, crushed notes, and diminutions. The memory of the ancient military formation is preserved in the alternation between festive themes and military themes signaling imminent danger. Similar groups are active in Isola del Gran Sasso and Castelli (Teramo).

12.2 Frame Drums (Tambourines)

Frame drums, also known as tambourines, are membranophones where the shell's height does not exceed the membrane's radius. The tambourine is the most widespread struck membranophone in Italy, especially in the central and southern regions, though it was also played in northern Italy, such as in Cogne (Valle d'Aosta) during the past century.

Tambourines come in various sizes, with the frame height generally proportional to the instrument's overall size. The number of jingles varies, usually arranged in pairs, often in odd numbers between three and nine, and mounted in single or double rows in the frame's slots (Fig. 54). In the area around Naples and in Calabria, jingles are often made from old tin cans.

Fig. 54 Tambourine with double row of jingles

The membrane is usually made of goat skin, but other animal skins like cattle, dog, cat, and rabbit are also used. The frame is typically made of beechwood, often crafted by the same artisans who make sieves. The technique for holding and playing the tambourine is generally consistent across Italy: one hand holds the frame, usually from underneath, and moves the instrument to make the jingles ring without striking the skin, while the other hand performs rhythmic sequences using various percussion techniques. Research shows that, unlike Italian tambourines, Islamic frame drums are alternately supported and struck by both hands (Guizzi, 2020).

There are different regional traditions in Italy regarding performance practices, but common principles include:

- Percussion with the palm of the hand
- Percussion with the edge of the hand

- Percussion with the fingertips held close together
- Percussion with the thumb and the knuckles

These techniques create sequences of long and short strokes, variously accented, repeated, and combined to produce the rhythmic basis for dance performances, enhanced by the jingles' tinkling.

12.2.1 Sicilian Tammureddu

The *tammureddu*, a tambourine kept in the Museum of Culture and Popular Music of the Peloritani, has a beechwood frame shaped like a circle with overlapping edges, painted green. The goat skin membrane is unpainted and glued to the frame. Four pairs of square tin jingles of different sizes, each with rounded edges, are housed in four slots along the frame. The instrument does not have a specific opening for holding (Fig. 55).

Fig. 55 Sicilian Tammureddu

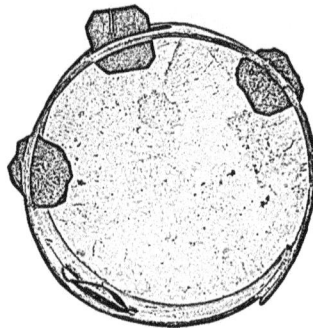

12.2.2 History of Sicilian Tammureddi

Research shows that *tammureddi* have been widely used in Sicily since the Middle Ages, though the earliest documents date back to the 16th century. One document from 1542 reports a partnership between priest Bernardo Gulino from Alcamo and painter Filippo Giuffrè to produce tambourines decorated with sacred images (Cataldo, 1997).

The fairs held during the local festivals honoring patron saints provided profitable opportunities for the sale of these instruments. For this reason, in the 15th and the 16th centuries, tambourine makers would increase their production several months before the most important festivals, aware that the fairs, which lasted several days, attracted hundreds of visitors and thus many potential buyers (Genzardi, 1891). Interestingly, throughout Sicily, sieve makers also built tambourines: the wooden frame was the same, but it was completed with a mesh when making a sieve or with a skin membrane when making a tambourine. A scholar estimates that tens of thousands of tambourines were produced between the 16th and the 17th centuries (Di Stefano, 2013).

Tambourines often featured metal jingles, which were sometimes circular, and the skins were painted with anthropomorphic subjects by professional painters (Di Stefano, 2013). Women were involved in both tambourine construction and performance, which was largely considered a female prerogative (Di Stefano, 2013).

Unfortunately, while many documents bearing witness to the history of the tambourine in Sicily have been preserved, few ancient tambourines have survived. A 17th-century tambourine membrane was found, separated from its frame and used about a century later to bind a notarial volume. Although the decoration is damaged, three dancing figures—two ladies and a knight—dressed in elegant 17th-century attire are still recognizable (Di Stefano, 2013).

12.2.3 Sardinian Tamburellu

The *tamburellu,* a tambourine from the Campidano area of Cagliari, where its use is being revived in folk music, has a circular wooden frame. The leather membrane is sewn or nailed to the frame and struck with the fingers. Rectangular slots in the frame hold jingles made of concave tin plates. Little bells are hung inside the *tamburellu* to enhance the jingles' tinkling sound (Fig. 56).

Fig. 56 Sardinian Tamburellu

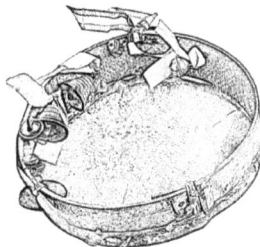

Current instruments are smaller than those used between the 19th and the early 20th centuries. Iconographic evidence shows that a larger tambourine, known as *su sizilianu* (the Sicilian), a name referring to its origin, was common in Sardinia during that period.

12.2.4 Abruzzese Ciciombre and Tamorra

In the Vestine area, there are two types of tambourines. The smaller- to medium-sized *ciciombre* has a beechwood frame and a donkey skin membrane. It is equipped with square jingles with rounded edges arranged in a single row, producing a rich and sharp sound due to the metal parts within the slots in which they are housed. The instrument does not have a specific opening for holding (Fig. 57).

Fig. 57 Abruzzese Ciciombre

The medium-to-large *tamorra* measures about 40 cm in diameter and 10 cm in height. It has a beechwood frame and a donkey skin membrane and lacks jingles.

12.3 Friction Drums

A friction drum is a single-membrane drum consisting of a container open at the top, with a membrane stretched over the opening. At the center of the membrane is a device (a vertically inserted stick or cord) that transmits impulses from the performer to the membrane. The performer rubs the stick or cord with their hand, which may be moistened or equipped with a wet cloth for a better effect (Fig. 58). The drum produces deep, short sounds characterized by a strong rhythmic drive, making it an essential component in dance accompaniment as well as in the production of sonorities imbued with ritual and symbolic meaning.

Fig. 58 Friction drum

Friction drums are referred to by a variety of names, often onomatopoeic, reflecting the sounds they produce: *cupa cupa* (Basilicata), *zuco zuco* (Calabria), *putipù* (Campania), *cuticù* (Latium), *firri firri* (Sicily), and *zumbu zumbu* (Sardinia). The term *caccavella* (meaning "clay pot"), used in Campania, instead refers to the vessel serving as the resonating chamber.

There are two types of friction drums: the stationary type, large and played with both hands together, featuring a long and thick stick as the vertical element, and the portable type. In the latter type, the instrument is held by the performer with one arm while the hand of the other arm rubs a shorter, thinner stick.

12.3.1 Molisano Bufù

In Molise, the *bufù*'s resonating body is typically made from a barrel, a small wine cask, or a vat used to collect grape must. The vertical element, whether a stick or a rod, is made from cane, with its thickness and length proportional to the instrument's size. It is attached to the membrane with a cord. The membrane is usually made from goat or lamb skin, with the fur facing inward toward the resonator (Fig. 59).

Fig. 59 Molisano Bufù

Ethnomusicologist Mauro Gioielli notes that the *bufù* is primarily played during *maitunate*—New Year's Eve Songs—as well as other rituals like Carnival and *Maggiolate*—May celebrations—held respectively in Casacalenda and San. Felice del Molise (Campobasso) (Gioielli, 1996).

12.3.2 Sardinian Trìmpanu

In Sardinia, there are several types of friction drums, with the *trìmpanu* (also called *zumbu zumbu*), being considered the most distinctive. Evidence of this instrument is found in the Barbagia region of Ollolai. It features a cylindrical shell made of tin or cork, with a membrane traditionally crafted from dog skin with a central hole. The hole is reinforced with two leather rings to prevent tearing. A string coated with tar passes through the hole, and the performer tightens it while sliding it between their fingers, causing the membrane to vibrate (Fig. 60).

Fig. 60 Sardinian Trìmpanu

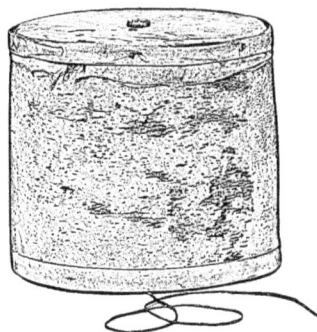

The performance technique requires the performer to initiate the sound-producing action by grasping the string at its base, which limits the creation of complex rhythmic patterns. It is believed that the *trìmpanu* was historically used to herd flocks and scare off predatory animals.

12.3.3 Abruzzese Bhù-Bbù, Vurre Vurre, Vurrecone, and Battefoche

In the Vestine area, single-headed friction membranophones come in various sizes: the *bbù-bbù* is the smallest instrument in the family (Fig. 61), with the *vurre vurre*, the *vurrecone*, and the *battefoche* (Fig. 62) being progressively larger, and the *battefoche* being the largest of them all. These instruments share similarities and specific differences: in both extremes, the membrane is made of donkey skin; the *bbù-bbù*'s shell is made of beechwood, while the *battefoche*'s shell is made of pressed cardboard. The vertical element is a wicker stick in the *bbù-bbù* and a cane stick in the *battefoche*.

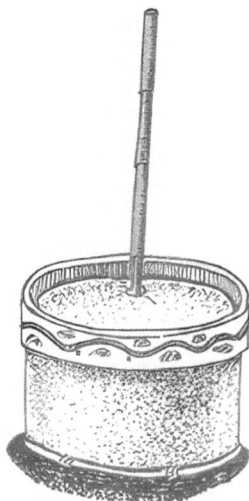

Fig. 61 Bbù-bbù   Fig. 62 Battefoche

Summary

Membranophones are musical instruments distinguished by the vibration of membranes stretched under tension. Within this class, two significant sub-classes are
discussed struck drums and friction drums. Struck drums include cylindrical drums
and frame drums (also termed tambourines). Among the cylindrical drums, this study
examines the Sicilian *tabbala* and *tammurinu*, the Sardinian *tamburu*, *tumbarinos*,
and *tumbarineddu*, as well as the Abruzzese drum. A specific section discusses
the ceremonial uses of drums in Sicily and in Abruzzo. Among the frame drums,
the analysis includes the Sicilian *tammureddu*, the Sardinian *tamburellu*, and the
Abruzzese *ciciombre* and *tamorra*. In the sub-class of friction drums, instruments
like the Molisano *bufù*, the Sardinian *trímpanu*, and several Abruzzese instruments
(*bbù-bbù*, *vurre vurre*, *vurrecone*, and *battefoche*) are explored.

Keywords

Abruzzese Drum, *Battefoche*, *Bbù-Bbù*, *Bordoniera*, *Bufù*, *Ciciombre*, Cymbals,
Frame Drums (Tambourines), Friction Drums, *Maitunate*, Membranophones,

Organettu, Pìffaru, Sa Cointrotza, Sardinian *Tamburellu*, Sardinian *Tumbarineddu*, Sicilian *Tammureddu*, Sicilian *Tammurinu*, *Su Sizilianu, Tabbala, Tamburu* from Sassari, *Tamorra, Triangulu, Trìmpanu, Tubbiana, Tumbarinu, Tumbarinu ʻe Gardone, Vurre Vurre, Vurrecone*.

Preeminent Figures

- Bernardo Gulino from Alcamo
- Filippo Giuffrè
- Mauro Gioielli

Questions for Review

1. What are membranophones, and what are two of their main sub-classes?
2. What is meant by cylindrical drums?
3. What materials can be used to make the shell of a cylindrical drum?
4. What distinguishes the *tumbarinu ʻe gardone* from other *tumbarinos*?
5. What is the *bordoniera*, and what is its function?
6. How is the skin of cylindrical drums tanned?
7. What is the purpose of the two different mallets used to play the *tumbarinu* from Aidomaggiore?
8. Which cylindrical drum is played without mallets?
9. What is the *Tubbiana*?
10. Which pieces are part of the traditional repertoire of *Li Tamurrë di Pretara*?
11. What is meant by frame drums (or tambourines)?
12. What was the primary activity of Sicilian tambourine makers?
13. What is meant by friction drums, and what are their main types?
14. On what occasions is the *bufù* primarily played?

Further Reading and Online Resources

Cataldo, Carlo. *I suoni sommersi: Musica, danza e teatro ad Alcamo*. Alcamo, Italy: Edizioni Campo, 1997.

Di Silvestre, Carlo. *Tradizioni musicali abruzzesi. Tamburi, pifferi e zampogne della Valle Siciliana*. Pineto, Italy: d'Abruzzo Libri, 1998.

Di Silvestre, Carlo. *Strumenti musicali di tradizione popolare*. Pineto, Italy: Il Passagallo, 2004.

Di Stefano, Giovanni Paolo. "Strumenti musicali nelle collezioni siciliane." In *Strumenti musicali in Sicilia*, edited by Giovanni Paolo Di Stefano, Selima Giorgia Giuliano, and Sandra Proto, 17–52. CRicd, Palermo, Italy: Regione Siciliana, 2013.

Genzardi, Bernardo. *Il Comune di Palermo sotto il dominio spagnuolo*. Palermo, Italy: Tipografia del Giornale di Sicilia, 1891.

Gioielli, Mauro. "Il bufù: appunti sulla tradizione del tamburo a frizione nel Molise." *Utriculus*, 18, April–June 1996: 34–41.

Guizzi, Fabio. *Guida alla musica popolare in Italia*. Lucca, Italy: LIM, 2020.

Pitrè, Giuseppe. *La casa, la famiglia, la vita*. Palermo, Italy: Il Pomerio, 1913.

CHAPTER 13

Chordophones

Chordophones are instruments in which one or more strings are stretched between fixed points.

13.1 Composite Chordophones

A sub-class of chordophones is that of composite chordophones, which scholars describe as instruments comprising a string support and a resonator that are permanently connected, making it impossible to separate them without destroying the sound apparatus (von Hornbostel, Sachs, and Guizzi, 2020). Lutes are part of this sub-class.

13.1.1 Colascione

The colascione is a particular type of lute used in traditional and folk music. The colascione (or *calascione*) is essentially a lute with a very long and slender neck, and a pear-shaped body, similar to that of a mandolin but smaller. It usually has three strings. Research suggests it may have originated from similar Turkish-Persian lutes known as the *saz* and the tanbur (Guizzi, 2020) (Fig. 63).

Additionally, a derivative of the colascione, called the *gallichone*, also spelled *galischona*, *galizona*, or *galischan*, was widely used in Europe in past centuries (Eglhuber, 2018). It fulfilled both a continuo role—evidenced by works of Johann Kuhnau and Georg Philipp Telemann (Schlegel, 2017)—and a melodic one, as demonstrated by a trio in C major for two *gallichons*, attributed to Placidus von Camerloher, an 18th-century Bavarian composer. There is extensive iconographic documentation of Italian colasciones, particularly those from northeastern Italy, Campania, and Sicily. Some artistically decorated colasciones are preserved in

Fig. 63 Colascione

musical instrument collections. Additionally, the use of a colascione in Castelpoto (Benevento) has been confirmed: it features an elongated body made from a single piece of wood, a neck slightly longer than the body, and three metal strings stretched by pegs set in a disc-shaped pegbox (Fig. 64).

The unique shape of the Benevento colascione suggests that the term *colascione* generally refers to a long-necked lute known in various forms.

Musical pieces, whether sung or purely instrumental, that are performed with the colascione are called *colascionate*. According to scholar Mauro Gioielli, in some areas of Latium, Abruzzo, Campania, and Sicily, the term *colascionata* referred to a love song performed with the accompaniment of the colascione (Gioielli, 2006). Other researchers note that this instrument was mainly used to accompany serenades (Guizzi, 2020), often of a melancholic nature, which the performer would sing in the evening under his beloved's window (Polce, 1924). An example of a *colascionata* is the song *Fenesta vascia* (Lowly window), subtitled *Colascionata napolitana* (Neapolitan song accompanied by the colascione),

Fig. 64 Colascione from Castelpoto

attributed to Guillaume Louis Cottrau but acknowledged by scholars as a popular song from the 16th century, simply arranged rather than composed by Cottrau.

Ethnomusicologist Gioielli also highlights that string production for musical instruments, including the colascione, was a traditional activity in the towns of Salle, Bolognano, and Musellaro (Pescara). Expert craftsmen from these towns went on to work in various Italian cities and even abroad, establishing a true school of art (Gioielli, 2006). The thriving production of strings for the colascione in Abruzzo suggests that the making of the finished instruments must also have been of considerable importance in the region.

Ethnologist Giuseppe Pitrè and writer Arturo Lancellotti explored a Palermo carnival tradition: small groups of musicians known as *pulcinelli*, equipped with colascione, *putipù*, and tambourine with jingles, would roam the city, stopping in front of shops such as fruit vendors, delicatessens, bakers, and inns. There, they performed praise songs for the shop managers, receiving money or edible gifts like bread, salami, fruit, and wine (Pitrè, 1870–1871; Lancellotti, 1951).

In Campania, the colascione was associated with dances, as evidenced by the engravings of Jacques Callot (1592–1635) in the book *I balli di Sfessania* [The Sfessania dances], published anonymously around 1622 (Fig. 65).

Fig. 65 Engraving from *I balli di Sfessania*

The *sfessania*, which gives the book its title, is considered by a scholar to be a Moorish-origin dance and a precursor to the tarantella (Confuorto, 2023). These engravings attest to the use of various musical instruments, including the colascione. Research has shown that in Naples, in the first half of the 1600s, the colascione was considered "*o Re de li stromiente*" (the King of all musical instruments) (Depalma, 2010).

An early 20th-century scholar, Italo Polce, reported that in 1923, during the event named *Settimana Abruzzese* (Abruzzese Week) in Castellammare Adriatico (now Pescara), *colascionari* (colascione players) from other parts of the region performed with great success, with one performer belonging to the group from Pratola Peligna (L'Aquila). The same article mentioned that although there were no virtuosos of this instrument in Castellammare Adriatico at that time, the memory of virtuosos from the previous generation was still vivid among the inhabitants of Abruzzo (Polce, 1924).

Currently, continuing a trend that has been ongoing for decades, the colascione is more frequently used in the context of early music than in traditional music.

Summary

Chordophones are instruments in which one or more strings are stretched between fixed points. A notable sub-class is that of composite chordophones, in which the instrument consists of a string support and a resonator, permanently connected so that they cannot be separated without destroying the sound-producing structure. Lutes fall under this sub-class. Among these, the colascione is prominent in traditional and folk music. The colascione is related to similar instruments found across Europe, known as *gallichone*, *galischona*, *galizona*, and *galischan*, that were used both for basso continuo and as melodic instruments. The colascione held a significant role in the performance of love songs, known as *colascionate*, during Palermo's carnival traditions and in the *sfessania* dance, a Moorish-origin dance that preceded the tarantella.

Keywords

Colascionata, Composite Chordophones, Chordophones, *Gallichone, Pulcinelli, Saz* and Tanbur, *Sfessania*.

Preeminent Figures

- Arturo Lancellotti
- Georg Philipp Telemann
- Giuseppe Pitrè
- Guillaume Louis Cottrau
- Jacques Callot
- Johann Kuhnau
- Mauro Gioielli
- Placidus von Camerloher

Questions for Review

1. What are chordophones, and more specifically, what are composite chordophones?
2. How is a colascione made?
3. Which composers wrote compositions for the *gallichone* between the 17th and the 18th centuries?

4. What specific construction features distinguish the Castelpoto colascione from those of other regions?
5. What are the *colascionate*?
6. What function did the *pulcinelli* have during the Palermo Carnival?
7. What is the *sfessania*?
8. In what contexts is the colascione used today?

Further Reading and Online Resources

Confuorto, Valentina. *I Balli di Sfessania, Storia, migrazioni e presenza teatrale di una danza moresca napoletana.* Roma: Bulzoni, 2023.

Depalma, Fedele. *'O re de li stromiente': il colascione nelle fonti musicali, letterarie e iconografiche.* Lecce, Italy: Grifo, 2010.

Eglhuber, Christoph. "Solo per la Gallichone: Zur Lautenmusik des Freisinger Hofkapellmeisters Placidus von Camerloher (1718–1782)." 2018. Accessed November 3, 2024. https://doi.org/10.15463/gfbm-mib-2018-223.

Gioielli, Mauro. "Quattro Colascionate." *Utriculus*, 39 (July–September), 2006: 19–39.

Guizzi, Fabio. *Guida alla musica popolare in Italia.* Lucca, Italy: LIM, 2020.

Lancellotti, Arturo. *Feste tradizionali.* Milano, Italy: Società Editrice Libraria, 1951.

Pitrè, Giuseppe. *Canti popolari siciliani*, 2 vols., I. Palermo, Italy: Pedone—Lauriel, 1870–1871.

Polce, Italo. "Il calascionaro." *Il risorgimento d'Abruzzo e Molise*, VI (388), January 17, 1924.

Schlegel, Andreas. "Colascione—Galizone—Mandora: Eine Klärung." *Lauten-Info der Deutschen Lautengesellschaft*, 3, 2017: 12–15.

von Hornbostel, Erich, Curt Sachs, and Febo Guizzi. "Classification of Musical Instruments." Translated by Anthony Baines and Klaus Wachmann. In *Reflecting on Hornbostel-Sachs's Versuch a Century Later: Proceedings of the International Meeting Venice, July 3–4, 2015*, edited by Cristina Ghirardini, 227–279. Venezia, Italy: Edizioni Fondazione Levi, 2020.

CHAPTER 14

Aerophones

Aerophones, the class numbered 4 in the Hornbostel-Sachs system, are instruments in which air is the primary medium that is set into vibration.

14.1 Free Aerophones

Within the class of aerophones, there is a sub-class known as free aerophones, where the vibrating air is not contained within the instrument. Among these, a category called interruptive aerophones consists of instruments that periodically interrupt the airflow.

14.1.1 Bullroarer

An example of a free aerophone that periodically interrupts airflow is the bullroarer. It consists of a light wooden board about 20 cm long with rounded edges, with a hole near one of the short ends, through which a thin string, about a meter long, is passed. The performer swings the bullroarer by holding the string and spinning the instrument in the air, generating pressure waves that are perceived as sound by a stationary listener (Fig. 66).

Fig. 66 Bullroarer

In Sicily, the bullroarer is called *lapuni* (meaning large bee), a term that alludes to its sound, similar to the buzzing of a large bee. In Sardinia, this instrument is designated by the onomatopoeic terms *frusciu* and *burriburri*.

14.2 Free Reed Aerophones

A reed is an elastic device made of one or two thin strips of wood or other material, which can be placed in a resonant cavity or attached to a sounding tube. When subjected to airflow, the reed vibrates, exciting the surrounding air and producing sound. When there is only one lamella, the reed is called single (Fig. 67); when there are two lamellae, placed close together and partially joined, the reed is called double (Fig. 68).

Fig. 67 Single reed   Fig. 68 Double reed

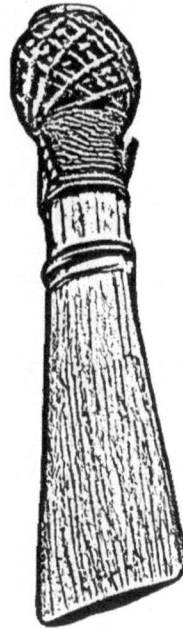

A single reed is called a beating reed if it strikes against a surface during its vibration, or a free reed if it is fixed to a frame at only one end and vibrates freely within the frame. A double reed is always a beating reed.

Among aerophones, some instruments use airflow forced against a series of free reeds and are equipped with a bellows to supply the air. This group includes the diatonic accordion and the bandoneon.

14.2.1 Diatonic Accordion

The diatonic accordion is a mechanical aerophone with free reeds, generally double-tuned. The term "mechanical" refers to the fact that the reeds vibrate not by the performer's breath but by air stored in a bellows, which is compressed and expanded to direct airflow to the reeds, causing them to vibrate.

14.2.1.1 Structure

The diatonic accordion is composed of three main parts: the bellows in the center and the treble casing and the bass casing on either side. The button keyboard is located on the outer end of the treble casing, with the reeds and valves housed inside it. A single valve supplies air to a pair of reeds: one reed vibrates when the bellows closes, and the other vibrates when the bellows opens. In the bass casing, there are accompaniment buttons, the related reeds and valves, and the "air button," which is used to empty the bellows (Fig. 69).

Fig. 69 Diatonic accordion: A. treble casing; B. bellows; C. bass casing; D. leather loop for the right thumb; E. strap for the left hand

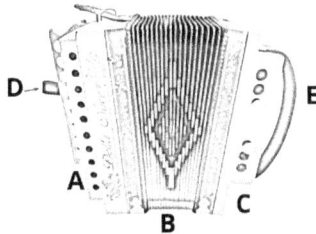

The reeds of the diatonic accordion are housed within wooden structures called soundboards (Fig. 70), mounted in two small wooden boxes.

Fig. 70 Soundboards

The first phase of reed construction is done by machine, and the finishing is completed by hand, with the goal of improving each reed's elasticity and sound quality.

Each reed consists of a thin steel strip, with one end fixed onto a perforated aluminum or brass plate, allowing the reed to be exposed to air and vibrate, producing sound (Fig. 71).

Fig. 71 Reed mounted on a plate

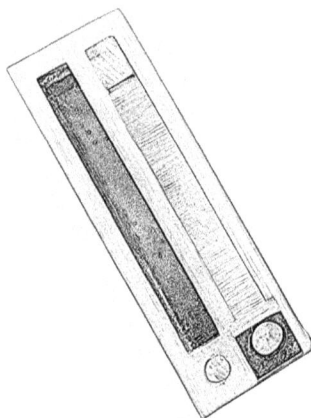

The plates are placed on the soundboard (Fig. 72) and secured with a synthetic resin, allowing for easy removal, maintenance, or replacement of the reed.

Fig. 72 Plates placed on the soundboard

Each plate has two reeds attached, one on each side of the plate, which vibrate according to the direction of the bellows. One reed vibrates when the bellows opens, as air is drawn in, and the other vibrates when the bellows closes, as air is compressed. The same principle applies to the harmonica, which produces different sounds when the performer inhales or exhales. To ensure that only one reed vibrates at a time in the diatonic accordion, a small strip of plastic or leather behind each reed acts as a stopper, preventing air from reaching that specific reed and setting it into vibration.

Most diatonic accordions are bisonoric, meaning that the two reeds mounted on the same plate and activated by the same button produce two different, usually adjacent, notes. This design helps keep the instrument compact. In contrast, in a unisonoric accordion, both reeds produce the same note, meaning that, for the same number of notes, the diatonic accordion is half the size of a standard accordion. There are also unisonoric diatonic accordions, which, like accordions, produce the same note regardless of how the bellows is used, and mixed diatonic accordions, which combine a bisonoric button panel with a unisonoric one.

The size of the reed determines the pitch of the note produced: for example, a smaller reed produces a higher-pitched note. The diatonic accordion is described as two-voice, three-voice, or four-voice, depending on the number of reeds sounding simultaneously. In the two-voice model, each note is produced by two reeds that can sound in unison or with slight dissonance between them (creating a tremolo effect) or an octave apart. In a four-voice diatonic accordion, there is one reed that produces the true note, one reed that produces the true note with slight dissonance (e.g., one tuned to 440 Hz and the other to 442 Hz), one reed that produces the octave above, and one that produces the octave below. By operating the registers, controlled by knobs or small levers, various combinations of reed sets corresponding to the same physical button or key on the instrument can be utilized, producing different sound effects for the same note.

The external parts of the diatonic accordion are commonly made of cherry, walnut, or olive wood, while beech and spruce are used for the internal components. The bellows is made of leather-board, which is cardboard made more elastic and durable by adding leather fibers. Leather joints ensure the connection of the bellows to the two casings.

Types of diatonic accordions are often distinguished by the number of bass or accompaniment buttons, which can range from as few as two, four, or eight, up to twelve or even twenty-four. The basic and most widely known model, widespread in central Italy, is called *a due bassi* (two-bass) (Fig. 73). Other common models include the four-bass version (Fig. 74), found mainly in Calabria, and the eight-bass version (Fig. 75), predominantly used in Sardinia.

Fig. 73 Two-bass diatonic accordion

Fig. 74 Four-bass diatonic accordion

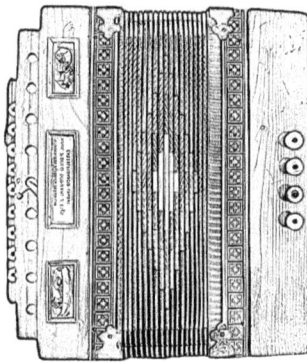

Fig. 75 Eight-bass diatonic accordion

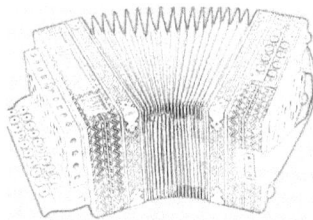

In Abruzzo, the version with only two bass buttons is called *ddu botte* (two knocks). Various hypotheses have been made about the origin of this name: it could derive from the movement the performer makes by extending and closing their arms to open and close the bellows, applying two firm pushes; alternatively, or perhaps complementarily, the term could also be related to the fact that, through the opening and closing of the bellows, the instrument respectively produces the dominant chord and the tonic chord.

The *ddu botte* has, on the treble casing, an outer row of nine buttons and an inner row of three smaller buttons called *vocette*. When the bellows closes, the nine buttons yield the notes of the tonic chord in the sequence V–I–III, meaning in a *ddu botte* in C, G–C–E–G–C–E–G–C–E. When the bellows opens, the nine buttons produce the notes of the sequence VII–II–IV–VI, that is, in a *ddu botte* in C, B–D–F–A–B–D–F–A–B. The *vocette* produce the notes D–F–A when the bellows closes, and the notes C–E–G when the bellows opens. Using all the buttons, the range of the instrument extends over more than two octaves. The keyboard on the treble casing is operated by the right hand of the performer, who can insert their right thumb into a leather loop positioned at the edge of the keyboard.

With the left hand, the performer plays the accompaniment keyboard, which has two buttons: the upper button produces chords (the tonic chord when the bellows closes and the dominant chord when the bellows opens), while the lower button produces single notes in the lower register (the tonic when the bellows closes, and the dominant when the bellows opens).

14.2.1.2 History

Some scholars believe that the diatonic accordion has a "relationship" with an ancient Chinese instrument, the *sheng*, a mouth organ with free reeds. The *sheng* is mentioned in a document dating back to 1100 BCE, but the first precise evidence is a depiction of the instrument on a votive stele from 551 CE, preserved at the University of Pennsylvania Museum of Archaeology and Anthropology (Gellerman, 1996).

The *sheng* consists of a round container, which serves as an air reservoir, and various tubes. Initially, the container was a small gourd, whose natural neck served as a mouthpiece and air conduit (Fig. 76). The *sheng* was brought to the West around 1170. Around 1750, the German musician Johann Wilde, who was one of the court musicians in St. Petersburg, acquired a *sheng* and learned to play it (Gellerman, 1996).

Fig. 76 Sheng

In 1829, Cyrill Demian patented an early accordion in Vienna. This instrument had five buttons, each capable of producing a chord (hence the name "accordion" given to the instrument), with reeds placed inside a box and made to vibrate by means of a bellows (Fig. 77). The instrument was well received and became widely popular in the Austrian Empire, and by the following year, it had also gained popularity in France.

Fig. 77 Cyrill Demian's accordion

As Demian's original accordion was gradually developed, with the addition of new buttons and improvements in the construction and control of the bellows, various variants of the instrument emerged. Among these, thanks to the contributions of other inventors and further innovations, the diatonic accordion was born.

The diatonic accordion initially spread among the cultured bourgeoisie of major European cities before gaining popularity in folkloric settings across Europe, thanks to its ease of use, pleasant tone, and ability to produce both melody and accompaniment. Later, as research has shown, the diatonic accordion enjoyed great success in folk environments across Europe, in both North and South America, and in Madagascar (Giannattasio, 1994).

Research has highlighted that for a long time, instruments considered an intermediate form between the diatonic accordion and the accordion were used, called "semi-chromatic accordions," characterized by chromatic basses and a diatonic melody section (Guizzi, 2020).

14.2.1.3 Distribution

In Italy, the diatonic accordion is mainly found in the central and southern regions, such as Latium, in the province of Rieti, where specific music festivals dedicated to this instrument are held. Additionally, the diatonic accordion is often included in the lineup of dance orchestras. In Molise, a large part of traditional music involves the use of the diatonic accordion. In Basilicata and Calabria, it is one of the favored instruments for performing tarantellas, while in Puglia, it is used for playing *pizzica* dances.

In Sicily, the diatonic accordion is known as *ogganettu*. An instrument built in Giarre (Catania) in 1930 has 19 buttons on the treble casing and 10 buttons on the bass casing. The perforated panels, screwed onto the casings, are particularly interesting, with about 60 holes artistically arranged in groups (Fig. 78).

Fig. 78 Sicilian ogganettu

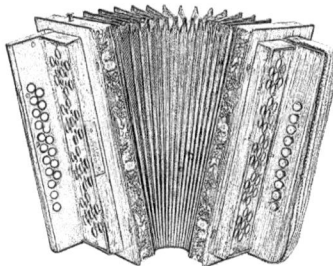

In Sardinia, where the presence of the diatonic accordion is attested almost everywhere, the instrument is known by the names *organette, organettu, organittu,* and *sonettu.* Typical accessories include the shoulder strap, which the performer passes over their right shoulder, and the hand strap, a ribbon usually made of leather, into which the performer inserts their left wrist, allowing them to operate the bellows without using their hand, which remains free to play the accompaniment (Fig. 79).

Fig. 79 Sardinian organette

Among the reasons for its widespread popularity in Sardinia, which began toward the end of the 19th century, are its pleasant tone, ease of handling, ease of playing, polyphonic nature, and its melodic, harmonic, and rhythmic possibilities. These qualities have made it a favored instrument for playing music originally intended for wind instruments, as well as for accompanying singing and dancing. The bass section of the diatonic accordion, for example, plays a fundamental role in emphasizing the metric structure of the composition, making it easier for dancers to perceive the pulse. The melodic lines are often enriched with ornamentation improvised on the spot.

Research has highlighted that in Sardinia, the most performed repertoire centers around dances, particularly those characteristic of specific territories. The diatonic accordion player is responsible for the unique dances of their community and therefore enjoys respect and esteem, especially if their performances are of a high artistic level (Giannattasio, 1994).

In the Grecanic area of Calabria (in the city and the province of Reggio Calabria), the two-bass diatonic accordion, known as *arganettu,* is widespread and is used to accompany traditional dances and songs. In addition to the southern regions, the diatonic accordion is also used in northwestern Italy and in Friuli, where instruments similar to those found in Austria and Slovenia are common. In Europe, it is widespread in Germany, France, Spain—particularly in the Basque Country—Sweden, and Ireland. In the latter country, a particular type of diatonic accordion with two rows of keys is popular. These rows of keys produce diatonic scales a semitone apart; however, to achieve the full chromatic scale, the performer must frequently change the direction of the bellows.

Outside Europe, the diatonic accordion is very popular in Brazil, where it is known as *gaita de botão* and is mainly used in Brazilian popular music.

Traditionally, the apprenticeship involved an extended phase of learning by imitation. A typical lesson consisted of several phases: the student would first listen to the various rhythmic-melodic sequences on which a piece was structured, one at a time, then alternate between listening and playing until they could perform all the sequences, and finally "sew" all the sequences together. In this learning method, memory obviously played a fundamental role.

14.2.1.4 Traditional Repertoire

The traditional repertoire consists of dance music (saltarellas, polkas, waltzes, mazurkas, and quadrilles), lyrical-monostrophic songs (such as serenades), narrative songs, and ritual songs associated with the collection of alms—for example, those performed during the feast of St. Anthony Abbot on January 17. Traditionally, all these pieces are passed down orally.

14.2.1.5 Revival

Since the 1950s, there has been a revival of traditional music, initially for cultural and political reasons: the aim was to rediscover the musical heritage of the subordinate classes. Then, in the 1980s, there was a revival of traditional dance: as a result, the diatonic accordion experienced a resurgence in popularity and saw renewed widespread use.

However, research has pointed out that revival practices differ from traditional ones in various aspects, such as:

- The area of distribution focuses primarily on the major cities of the central-northern regions.

- The transmission ceases to be exclusively oral; notation is also used, sometimes according to the tablature system.
- After an initial phase, in which the repertoire was limited to traditional pieces, works from foreign repertoires and newly composed pieces were gradually added.
- The expansion of the repertoire has led to an expansion of traditional performance techniques, achieved both by adopting performance techniques from other countries and by developing entirely new techniques (Tombesi and Tesi, 1993).

Interest in the diatonic accordion has led to the creation of special sections in folk music magazines and even specialized periodicals, such as *Anche Libre* (published in France) and *Diatonisch Nieuwsblad* (published in the Netherlands).

14.2.1.6 Similarities and Differences Between Diatonic Accordion and Bandoneon

Both the diatonic accordion and the bandoneon are portable aerophones with free reeds and bellows. They are composed of a treble casing and a bass casing, each containing a series of free reeds inside, and these casings are connected by a bellows, which acts on both simultaneously (Fig. 80). Unlike the diatonic accordion, where the performer's left hand can produce chords by pressing just a single button, the bandoneon requires both hands to operate buttons that produce single notes. The distinct organological characteristics of the two instruments shape the diversity of their respective repertoires and socio-musical functions.

Fig. 80 Bandoneon

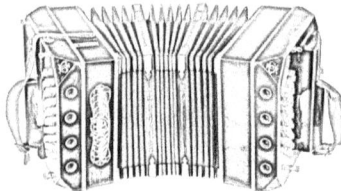

Regarding the repertoire, it is worth noting that the bandoneon, invented in Germany in 1845, arrived in Argentina and Uruguay between the late 19th and the early 20th centuries, and was incorporated into musical groups that played during dance parties. Over time, these musical groups focused their repertoire on an emerging musical genre, tango, for which the bandoneon became an essential instrument. The bandoneon is substantially larger in size, especially when compared to the *ddu botte*; the different structure naturally has a significant impact on the distinctly different timbre of the two instruments. While the diatonic accordion has only one hand strap, into which the performer inserts the wrist of their left hand, the bandoneon has two straps, one for each hand. The bandoneon player inserts their hands into the straps, each of which is attached to the outer side of a casing, so that the strap wraps around the metacarpal area, leaving the fingers free. The thumbs remain outside the straps and are used to maintain grip on the instrument.

There are essentially two types of bandoneons: the diatonic bandoneon and the chromatic bandoneon. As with the buttons of the bisonoric diatonic accordion, many buttons on the diatonic bandoneon produce different notes depending on whether the performer opens or closes the bellows when pressing the button. It should be noted that in the diatonic bandoneon, the arrangement of the buttons does not follow the chromatic pattern; instead, the arrangement often follows the principle of triads. For example, the buttons under three adjacent fingers might produce the notes of the A-flat major chord (A flat–C–E flat) when the bellows closes, and the notes of the diminished G chord (G–B flat–D flat) when the bellows opens. This arrangement facilitates the production of chordal harmonies but makes it rather difficult to play scales. To address this issue, bandoneon makers have developed a different model of the instrument, the chromatic bandoneon.

The chromatic bandoneon (or Kusserow system) is unisonoric, meaning it produces the same note whether the bellows opens or closes. The button layout is chromatic, and the positions are very similar to those used on the accordion.

The performer's position also differs between the diatonic accordion and the bandoneon: while the diatonic accordion is typically played standing, the development of additional buttons made the bandoneon heavier, making it easier to play while seated, with the instrument resting on the performer's legs. Later, some bandoneonists adopted the practice of playing while standing, resting the instrument on a semibent leg supported by a chair or tall stool.

Finally, in terms of formal education, research has shown that while academic courses for the diatonic accordion were introduced in Italian conservatories only after 2000, the Municipal Conservatory of Buenos Aires was offering regular bandoneon courses by 1950 (Salton, 1981).

14.3 Straight Flutes (Recorder Flutes)

Among aerophones, there is the sub-class of wind instruments proper, which comprises edge instruments including recorder flutes. Recorder flutes are documented throughout Italy and are made from different materials, such as cane (*Arundo donax*), elder or willow wood, sheep bone, goat horn, or the bark of chestnut, willow, or ash. Straight flutes can have the mouth permanently blocked with wooden or cork blocks, or a mixture of beeswax, oil, and tar, or they can have a temporary block made by the performer's tongue. The function of the block is to allow the blown air to split on the sharp edge (labium) of the window (Fig. 81).

Fig. 81 Head of a recorder: A. block; B. windway; C. labium

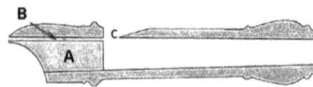

14.3.1 Calabrian Fischiottu

The double Calabrian flute (*fischiottu, fiscaruolu*) is an instrument mainly played and made by bagpipers, used similarly to the melodic pipes of the bagpipe. It consists of a pair of recorder flutes held simultaneously in the mouth, with the performer's hands operating each respective tube. Made of cane, double Calabrian flutes come in different sizes. The two main types are *fischiotti a paru*, with equal-length tubes held parallel, and *fischiotti a mezzachiave*, with one tube longer and wider than the other, held in a divergent position. Sometimes, three *fischiotti* are used together, with the third serving as a drone (Gatto, 2007) (Fig. 82).

Fig. 82 Calabrian fischiottu

14.3.2 Sicilian Friscalettu

In Sicily, the typical recorder flute is called *friscalettu*, *frautu*, or *farautu*, and is made from a segment of cane. A scholar has highlighted that for the construction of this type of musical instrument, canes of the species *Arundo donax* grown on dry soils are preferred (Sarica, 2004). The *friscalettu* can be cut in different pitches and is a very versatile instrument.

The occasions for its use are both traditional—such as agropastoral events like grape harvest and sheep shearing, and religious festivals—and focused on the revival of musical folklore. Today, the usual repertoire of the *friscalettu* is less focused on traditional dances than it once was, and it mostly includes modern dances such as waltzes, polkas, mazurkas, and tarantellas, which can also be performed with the accompaniment of tambourine, guitar, diatonic accordion, or accordion. The growing interest in the *friscalettu* has led to the publication of learning methods, something entirely unusual until recently, guiding beginners in techniques and performance practices. An example of this is the book by Gemino Calà (2001).

The *friscalettu* preserved in the Regional Interdisciplinary Museum of Messina comes from the eastern part of Sicily, near Messina, and dates back to the early 19th century. It is a straight cane flute characterized by a block probably made of oleander wood, and features both sacred and profane engravings. Among these is an engraving of St. Agatha, depicted with the classic symbols of martyrdom: the cross, the gospel, the crown, and the palm of martyrdom. The depiction of this saint on an instrument found near Messina suggests that devotion to St. Agatha, the patroness of Catania, was also widespread in Messina.

Other engravings on the front include a large eagle, while the back side features St. Peter and St. Paul, two knights with their horses near a fountain, and a depiction of the Annunciation. Additionally, there are various motifs inspired by architectural elements, including the frame of a Renaissance-style window, which, fittingly, frames the window of the *friscalettu* (Fig. 83).

The *friscalettu* preserved in the Giuseppe Pitrè Sicilian Ethnographic Museum in Palermo comes from eastern Sicily and is dated to the second half of the 19th century. It is made of cane, has a wooden block, and a rectangular window. The body of the flute is decorated with knife engravings depicting geometric motifs, a train, houses, and churches. The sounds produced form a D major scale, but it is also possible to obtain a natural F and a natural C.

Fig. 83 Friscalettu

The *friscalettu* preserved in the Museum of Popular Culture and Music of the Peloritani near Messina comes from the Peloritani Mountains area and is dated to the first half of the 20th century. It is a straight cane flute with an oleander wood block and a rectangular window, characterized by pastoral knife engravings, known as *riccami*, tinged with traces of red color (Fig. 84).

Fig. 84 Friscalettu

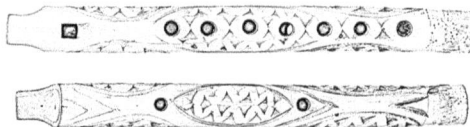

14.3.3 Pipiolu from the Logudoro region

Pipiolu is one of the names recorded in Sardinia for various types of straight flutes. The *pipiolu* from the Logudoro region (an instrument that is widespread in an area larger than just Logudoro) is a cane flute, made from a piece of cane that has, approximately in the middle of its length, a node that is either completely or partially pierced. The position of the node determines the position of the holes: the three front holes are located below the node, while the rear hole is located above it. The mouthpiece has a pronounced angle, and the window is rectangular in shape. The instrument is made in different sizes. The block is made of soft wood or sometimes cork (Fig. 85).

Fig. 85 Pipiolu from the Logudoro region

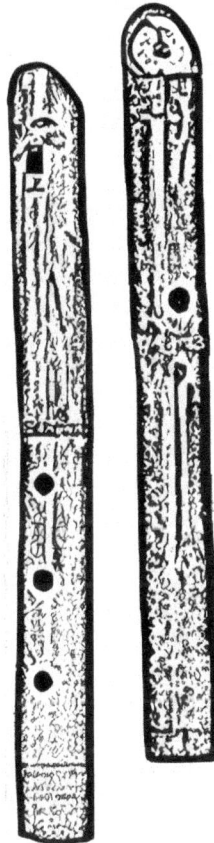

14.3.4 Pipaiolu from the Barbagia region

The straight flute known as *pipaiolu* from the Barbagia region is a cane flute made from a piece of cane with no intermediate nodes. All four holes are positioned on the front. The mouthpiece has a less pronounced angle than that of the *pipiolu* from the Logudoro region and the *sulittu* from the Marmilla region, and the window is rectangular and rather wide. The block is made of cork (Fig. 86). The instrument is made in different sizes and is often used, along with a drum, a triangle, and a diatonic accordion, to accompany dances. The rhythmically well-defined music guides and supports the dancers in performing the steps of various dances.

Fig. 86 Pipaiolu from the Barbagia region

14.3.5 Sulittu from the Marmilla region

Current research considers the *sulittu* from the Marmilla region a variant of the *pipiolu* from the Logudoro region (Spanu, 2008). The material used for its construction is cane, and the block is made of wood. It has four holes on the front and one hole on the back. Its main characteristic is that the hole in the back is not used to produce additional notes by facilitating the emission of higher harmonics, but rather to allow for easier fingering. The *sulittu* is made in different sizes (Fig. 87). For its construction, canes are collected in the winter months and seasoned for at least two years.

Fig. 87 Two specimens of sulittu from the Marmilla region

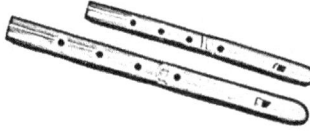

14.3.6 Sulittu and Tamburinu

Research has shown that the pairing of a long straight flute and a small double-headed cylindrical drum, both played by a single performer, was traditional in Sardinia (particularly in the Campidano region), as well as in the Spanish regions of the Basque Country and Catalonia, the French regions of Roussillon and Provence, and in the UK (Fara, 1940, 1997; Guizzi, 2020). Considering that these instruments were used simultaneously by a single performer, the *sulittu* and *tamburinu* pair is regarded as a single instrument, classified among the aerophones due to the predominant role attributed to the *sulittu*.

The *sulittu* is made of elderwood and has three holes: two on the front and one on the back; the *tamburinu* has a spruce wood shell, a sheepskin membrane, and is played with a small mallet rounded at the ends. A cord (*bordoniera*) is placed diametrically across the lower membrane and can be tightened by turning a wooden peg.

The performer held the *sulittu* with the left hand and played the melody using the first three fingers. A strap allowed the *tamburinu* to be hung from the left forearm, while the right hand struck its membrane with the mallet (Fig. 88).

Fig. 88 Sulittu and tamburinu

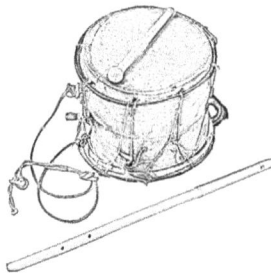

The *sulittu* and *tamburinu*, no longer in use today, played a significant role in accompanying dances and paraliturgical rites, such as the processions of confraternities. This is evidenced by various iconographic sources, including the painted panel by the Master from Castelsardo, which depicts a musical angel, the bas-relief from the Church of St. Bachisio in Bolotana (Nuoro), dating back to the 16th century, and several prints and paintings from the 19th century.

This instrument was widely popular in the Middle Ages, favored for its ease of use by musicians performing in the streets and taverns, as it allowed them to simultaneously play melody and rhythmic accompaniment. Ethnomusicologist Guizzi highlights that the continued presence of the instrument in Sardinia was most likely due to the influence of Catalan culture, particularly in the northwestern areas of the region (Guizzi, 2020).

14.3.7 Abruzzese Chioffërë

In Abruzzo, research has identified the use of a bone flute known as *chioffërë*, which is typical of the pastoral environment. This is evidenced by the fact that a sedentary form of pastoralism is practiced in its area of distribution (Macchie di Farindola, in the province of Pescara, and Befaro, a hamlet of Castelli, in the province of Teramo) (Di Silvestre, 2004). Traditionally, the *chioffërë* was played by shepherds once they had arrived at the pasture with their flock, during moments of rest and relaxation. For its construction, a goat or sheep femur is used, which is soaked for a few days and then stripped of marrow and spongy tissue. The most even outer side forms the front of the instrument, where a window and four holes are cut, while another hole is drilled on the back. A block made of beeswax, oil, and tar is then inserted at the upper end.

14.4 Bag Aerophones

In the class of aerophones, a sub-class is represented by wind instruments proper, including reedpipes. Among these are bag aerophones, instruments in which pipes and drones are supplied with air from a reservoir contained in a bag.

14.4.1 Origins

Research has not yet definitively clarified the origin of bag aerophones. While Baines cites passages from the comedies *The Acharnians* and *Lysistrata* by the

5th-century-BCE Greek playwright Aristophanes (1901), which contain descriptions that could suggest bag aerophones (Baines, 1960), Sachs, on the other hand, writes that the origin of the bagpipe is unknown (Sachs, 1940). It is known that in ancient times there were wind instruments such as the aulos and the *tibia*, for which performers had to practice specific techniques to make effective use of the air at their disposal. As a result, techniques like circular breathing were developed, and at some point, the idea likely arose to create an air reservoir that could be used when the performer needed to take a breath, allowing the sound to remain uninterrupted. Thus, a bag was applied to the instrument; this bag could then be connected to the sounding pipes (chanters and drones), continuously supplying them with air.

Scholar Febo Guizzi reports that the first instrument equipped with an air reservoir probably originated in the Indian region. The innovation involved placing a flexible air reservoir between the performer's mouth and lungs, on one side, and reedpipes like clarinets and oboes, on the other. This reservoir allowed the performer not only to have enough air to feed the reeds during breaths but also to simultaneously supply multiple pipes. The pipes need to have reeds, as the reeds act as valves that interrupt the air flow at specific temporal intervals, regulating the passage of air from the bag to the pipes. The application of the bag to different reed pipes already in use led to the development of various types of bag aerophones in different regions, inhabited by populations with distinct cultures (Guizzi, 2020).

14.4.2 From the 1st Century CE to the 20th Century

Curt Sachs reports that the first bag aerophone with reliable historical evidence dates to the 1st century CE (Sachs, 1940). This coincides with some documents from imperial Rome. One such testimony is provided by the poet Marcus Valerius Martialis (ca. 40–104), who, in his *Epigrams*, refers to a performer using a term of Greek origin, *ascaules* (Martial, 2008). In Greek, *ascos* referred to a bag, and aulos designated a wind instrument, presumably equipped with a reed. Therefore, the term *ascaules* likely referred to a performer who used an instrument with a bag and one or more reed-equipped pipes—essentially a bagpipe.

The historian and biographer Gaius Suetonius Tranquillus, who lived between the 1st and the 2nd centuries CE, mentioned that Emperor Nero (37–68 CE) played the *utriculus* (bagpipe) as a pastime (Suetonius, 2011). Similarly, the writer Dio Chrysostom (ca. 40 CE–after 112 CE), in a passage from his 71st oration, probably referring to Nero, stated that the emperor played the aulos while simultaneously compressing a bag with his arm (Chrysostom, 1951).

Unfortunately, no images from that period depicting the *utriculus* have survived. However, we have representations of this instrument, ideally related to the era of ancient Rome but created several centuries later. Examples include:

1. Francesco Bianchini's work, *De tribus generibus instrumentorum musicae veterum organicae dissertatio* [Dissertation on the Three Types of Musical Instruments Used in Instrumental Music of the Ancients], which contains two images of Roman bagpipes. One depicts an instrument with *tibiae pares* (pipes of the same length) arranged divergently, each with three holes and terminating in a bell; drones are not visible. The other shows an instrument with a single melody pipe with three holes and two drones of equal length, arranged parallel to each other and inserted separately from the melody pipe (Bianchini, 1742) (Fig. 89).

Fig. 89 Roman bagpipes

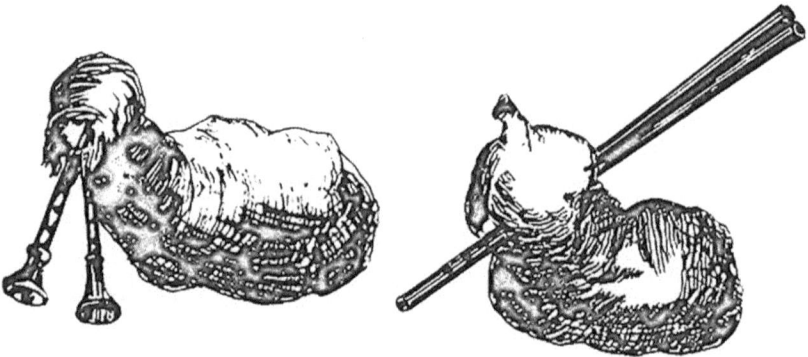

2. The work of Orazio Maccari, titled *Dissertazione sopra un'antica statuetta di marmo rappresentante un suonatore di cornamusa* [Dissertation on an Ancient Marble Statuette Representing a Bagpipe Player], depicts a bagpipe with a single chanter (Maccari, 1758) (Fig. 90).

Fig. 90 Ancient marble statuette described by Maccari

The archbishop Rabanus Maurus (780–856), in his *De Universo* [On the Universe], describes an aerophone called *chorus*, equipped with a leather bag and two pipes: one is the blowpipe, or insufflation pipe, through which the bag is inflated, and the other is a melody pipe that produces sound. Therefore, this *chorus* can be considered a rudimentary type of bagpipe without a drone (Maurus, n.d.).

Building on these accounts, organology scholar Anthony Baines suggests that the idea of using a bag to supply air to reedpipes began to spread just before the 13th century, experiencing rapid diffusion in Europe during the second half of the 13th century and the following century. Over time, this gave rise to a wide variety of instruments based on similar construction techniques (Baines, 1960). Given the widespread use of bag aerophones, it is unsurprising that, as research highlights, they appear in numerous works of visual art, many of which were religious in nature and produced in Italy (Staiti, 1997).

Furthermore, numerous literary references mentioning pivas and other types of bagpipes, dating from the 14th to the 17th centuries, have reached us. Among the authors who cite these instruments are Dante Alighieri in his *Divine Comedy*, Giovanni Boccaccio in his *Decameron*, Angelo Poliziano in his *Stanze* and *Favola d'Orfeo* [The Tale of Orpheus], Luigi Pulci in his *Morgante*, Torquato Tasso in his *Aminta*, Giambattista Marino in his works *Adone* and *Sampogna*, and Giambattista Basile in *Lo cunto de li cunti* [Tale of Tales]. On the one hand, it is necessary to bear in mind, as scholar Mauro Gioielli argues, that due to the generic and nonscientific names of the instruments, it is not unquestionably certain that these poets and writers were always referring to bagpipe aerophones in their writings (Gioielli, 1999).

On the other hand, it is noteworthy that so many prominent authors mention these instruments. The use of names such as piva, zampogna, *ciaramella*, and *cornamusa* in literary works suggests that bagpipe aerophones were becoming increasingly prominent in the musical landscape, to the point of being familiar even to nonspecialists.

Moreover, the existence of numerous instruments of this type suggests that luthiers were refining their construction techniques. As is well known, more sophisticated instruments enable the performance of a broader repertoire.

One of the most interesting innovations of the early 16th century was the production in Italy of the first bagpipe equipped with a bellows. In this instrument, the bag is inflated by the performer not by blowing into a blowpipe, but by operating a bellows connected to the bag. The first instrument of this kind was the *phagotus*, invented by Afranio degli Albonesi in the early 16th century (Albonesi, 1539) (Fig. 91).

Fig. 91 Phagotus

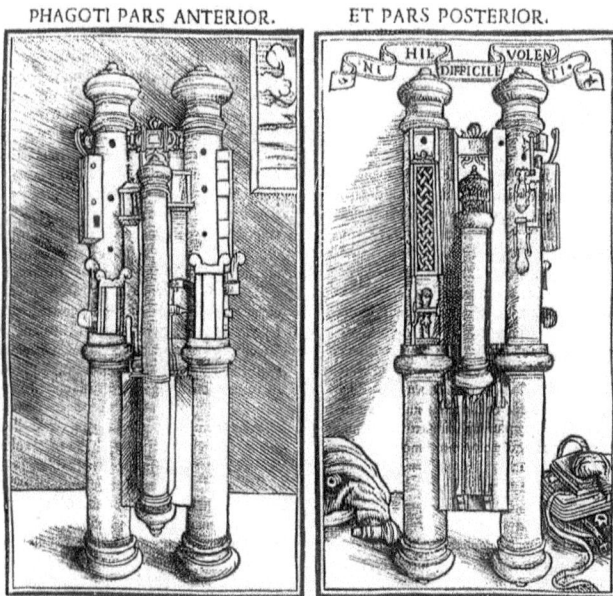

Among the 17th-century works that describe bagpipes is the *Syntagma musicum* by Michael Praetorius, a scholar mentioned in Chapter 4 as a precursor of ethno-organology (Praetorius, 1619) (Fig. 92).

Fig. 92 Bagpipe described by Praetorius

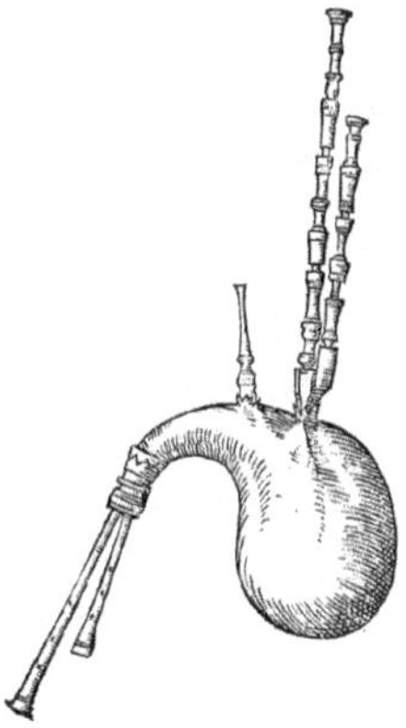

In the same Chapter 4, an important work by Marin Mersenne, *Harmonicorum instrumentorum libri IV*, was also mentioned. In this work, an illustration depicts an instrument that closely resembles certain types of southern Italian bagpipes and is equipped with a key on the right chanter (Mersenne, 1636: II, 92). This is the first time that such a device is mentioned in an organological study, referencing its presence in an Italian bagpipe used by performers from the lower classes (Fig. 93).

Fig. 93 Bagpipe described by Mersenne

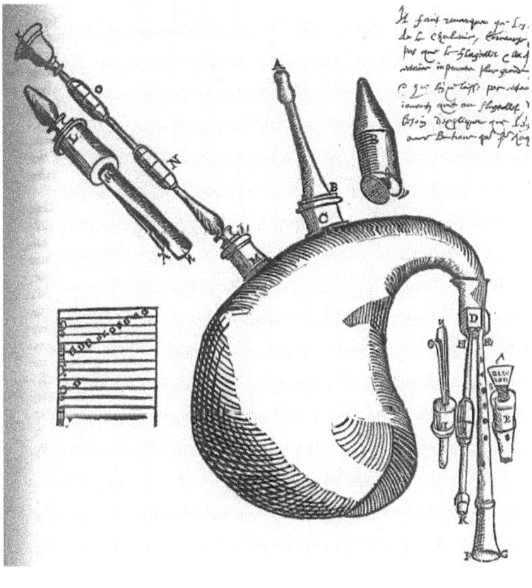

In the 18th century, Bonanni's *Gabinetto Armonico Pieno d'Istromenti Sonori, Indicati e Spiegati* [Musical Cabinet Full of Sounding Instruments, Shown and Explained] was published. This treatise describes numerous instruments and complements the descriptions with excellent engravings of the instruments discussed (Bonanni, 1722). Notably, the instruments Bonanni focuses on are of various types: popular music instruments, art music instruments, sound toys, and hunting calls, originating from Europe as well as Africa, Asia, and the Americas.

Bonanni's interest in musical instruments began in 1698, the year he succeeded Father Athanasius Kircher as curator of the museum of the Collegio Romano. This museum was established in 1651 by the Jesuits following a donation of curiosities by Italian antiquarian Alfonso Donnini. Kircher expanded the collection, adding objects of natural history, various machines, and musical instruments. Many of these "curiosities" were sent by Jesuit missionaries from distant lands. It is no coincidence that Kircher was mentioned in Chapter 4 as one of the precursors of ethno-organology.

The *Gabinetto Armonico* is particularly famous for its illustrations, created from engravings by the Dutch artist Arnold van Westerhout (1651–1725). Entries XXX and XXXI describe the piva (Fig. 94) and the *musetta* (Fig. 95), respectively.

Fig. 94 Piva described by Bonanni

xxx   *Piua o Ciaramella*

According to Bonanni's presentation, the first is a "customary instrument played by shepherds, commonly called Piva, by some Cornamusa, or indeed Ciaramella" (Bonanni, 1722: 73).

Fig. 95 Musetta described by Bonanni

XXXI   *Muſetta*

The second is "another similar instrument recently invented and used in France." Regarding the *musetta*, Bonanni writes that air is supplied to the bag by means of a bellows, allowing the performer to avoid "the effort of inflating it with their own breath, as the peasant does with the Piva" (Bonanni, 1722: 75).

In the 19th century, Romanticism emerged and spread as a cultural movement that expressed particular interest in the cultures and folklore of various peoples, contrasting with the internationalism of the Enlightenment. For Romanticism, traditional and popular music became highly significant as an expression of national culture. Studying and performing popular repertoires was considered an act of cultural patriotism. In line with this new perspective, even art music composers and musicologists began to show greater interest in the songs and instruments of popular music.

Among the composers of art music fascinated by popular instruments was Hector Berlioz, who documented his impressions of a trip to Italy in *Voyage musical en Allemagne et en Italie. Etudes sur Beethoven, Gluck et Weber. Mélanges et Nouvelles* [Musical Journey in Germany and Italy. Studies on Beethoven, Gluck, and Weber. Miscellanies and News]. In this work, he describes *pifferai* (*piffero* players) and *zampognari* (zampogna players) from Abruzzo playing while walking through the streets of Rome (Berlioz, 1844). As itinerant musicians, *zampognari* and *pifferai* exemplify the spontaneous naturalness that was seen as a key aspect of the popular spirit.

Further images of *zampognari* can be found in Hans Geller's volume *Die Bildnisse der deutschen Künstler in Rom, 1800–1830* [Portraits by German Artists in Rome, 1800–1830], published in 1952. The book features paintings and engravings by German artists who were active in Rome during the early 19th century. No fewer than 22 prints depict *zampognari*, documenting various models of the zampogna in use during that period (Geller, 1952) (Fig. 96).

Fig. 96 Zampogna player depicted by a 19th-century German artist

In the 19th century, photography emerged, and with the spread of this new technique after 1850, a considerable number of photographs capturing *zampognari* were taken. Compared to paintings, photographs are likely more true-to-life, whereas artists may have added imaginative details to make their paintings appear more exotic or picturesque.

Notable works discussing the zampogna, published between the late 19th and the early 20th centuries, include those by Victor Mahillon (1880–1892), Curt Sachs (1913), Erich von Hornbostel and Curt Sachs (1914), and André Schaeffner (1936). These studies were mentioned in Chapter 7.

Around 1877, the phonograph was invented, which later enabled Béla Bartók and Zoltán Kodály to record folk songs in the Hungarian countryside. It is well known that Bartók, whose studies were mentioned in Chapter 4, collected many pieces for traditional Hungarian instruments, several of which were for bagpipes.

In the early 1960s, the English scholar Anthony Baines published an in-depth study focused on bagpipe aerophones, with particular attention on the zampogna with key (Baines, 1960).

14.4.3 Italian Piva and Zampogna Bagpipes

Today in Italy, various types of bagpipe aerophones exist, each characteristic of a specific region and distinguished by differences in size, range, number of pipes, and construction materials—factors that shape the unique timbre of each instrument. The first major distinction to be made is between northern piva and southern zampogna bagpipes. Although this book focuses on the instruments of southern Italy, comparing the northern piva and the southern zampogna bagpipes is relevant, particularly in terms of their construction features and contexts of use.

14.4.3.1 Northern Italian Piva Bagpipes

In general, northern pivas bagpipes have the following characteristics:

- There are multiple openings in the bag where the sounding pipes are inserted.
- In many types, there is a single chanter, which the performer plays with both hands.
- The chanter has a double reed, while the drone has a single reed; this is often referred to as a "mixed reed setup."
- The bag is mouth-blown using an insufflation tube.

Unfortunately, there is limited information on the repertoire of northern pivas. Regarding iconographic sources, it is worth noting that the piva has often been depicted in Arcadian landscapes portraying idealized pastoral settings, where perfect and lasting happiness was envisioned. An example is the painting by Pietro Melchiorre Ferrari, *Frugoni in Arcadia*, dating back to the late 18th century, which shows the poet Carlo Innocenzo Frugoni reciting his verses, surrounded by members of the aristocracy dressed as shepherds and shepherdesses. In the foreground, a piva is depicted resting on the ground. Among the northern Italian pivas notable examples include:

1. **The *Baghet* from Lombardy and the *Baga* from Veneto:** Both names derive from *baga*, a word in the local dialect meaning "bag"; therefore, the diminutive *baghet* refers to the small size of the bag. The bag is made from sheep or goat skin. The *baghet* has a conical chanter with a double reed, featuring seven front holes and one rear hole. The two drones are cylindrical, each fitted with a single reed; the smaller drone is tuned an octave below the chanter, while the larger one is tuned two octaves lower (Fig. 97). The *baghet* is used to accompany dances and songs and was regularly played during festivities throughout the year. The oldest iconographic source depicting the *baghet* is a fresco from 1347, *Albero del Bonaventura* (Bonaventura's Tree), located in the Church of Santa Maria Maggiore in Bergamo.

Fig. 97 Baghet

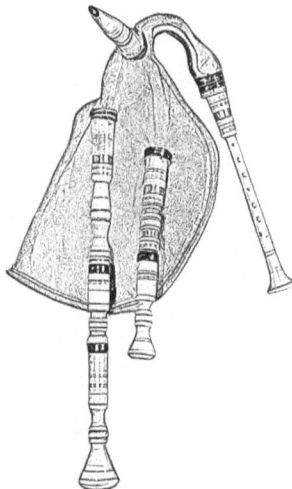

2.   **The Istrian Piva**, characteristic of Veneto and Istria: It has double chanters, each with a single reed, and lacks drones. Scholars have noted that the traditional repertoire of the Istrian piva was primarily centered around pieces played during wedding celebrations, from the bride's departure from her parents' house to the couple's exit from the church at the end of the ceremony, through the banquet (with a specific piece for each course), and concluding with the final dance (Dlačić and Badurina, 2012).

3.   **The *Musa/Müsa,*** known as "from the Four Provinces" of Alessandria, Genoa, Pavia, and Piacenza: It has a conical chanter with a double reed and seven front holes, and a cylindrical drone with a single reed. The drone consists of two sliding segments, allowing for pitch adjustment. Small lateral holes in the terminal segment of the drone can be left open or closed with wax or wooden blocks to alter the drone note (Fig. 98). The performer plays the chanter with both hands, while the drone rests against their left elbow. It is typically played in tandem with the folk oboe known as *piffero*, which plays the main melody, although scholars have suggested that, in some ancient dances, the *müsa* may have also performed solo sequences (Nastasi and Capezzuoli, 2010).

Fig. 98 Musa/müsa from the Four Provinces

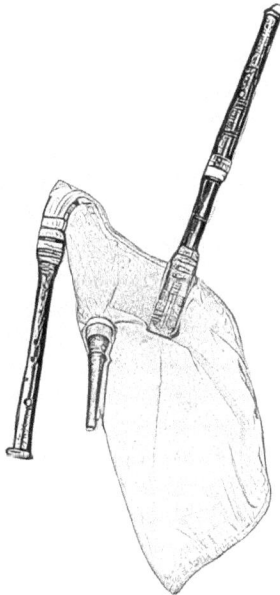

4. **The Piva from Emilia-Romagna** is a solo instrument with a chanter that has seven front holes and no rear hole. It has two drones producing notes one and two octaves below the chanter, respectively. The chanter, drones, and blowpipe are inserted separately into the bag (Fig. 99). In the Emilian piva, the shorter drone hangs beside the performer's right forearm, while the longer one rests on their left shoulder.

Fig. 99 Piva from Emilia-Romagna

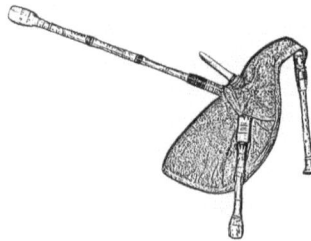

14.4.3.2 Southern Italian Zampogna Bagpipes

Several scholars believe that the name "zampogna" derives from the Greek *symphonia*, meaning "sounds together," and thus consonance, concert, or harmony (Gala, 2007; Sannino, 2017). It is worth noting that the term *zampoña* in Spanish refers to the Pan flute, typical of the Andean region. The connection suggested by the shared name between these different instruments may lie in the similarity between the pipes of the Pan flute and the sounding pipes of the bagpipe. According to another, perhaps more imaginative scholar, the term "zampogna" may derive from the Italian *zampona*, the augmentative form of *zampa* (paw), thus meaning "large paw" (Gioielli, 1995).

The zampogna, whose bag is usually made from goat or sheep skin, can symbolize the animal from which it originated, "coming to new life" through the sounds the instrument produces. If we imagine the bag as the animal's body, the chanters and drones could represent the legs of the beast, which is "brought back to life." The materials used to construct the zampogna may have influenced its traditional use in specific ritual contexts. Interestingly, in some areas of Latium and Molise, the natural leather bag has sometimes been replaced by pieces of inner tubes from car or truck tires, later covered with wool or fabric.

In general, southern zampogna bagpipes have the following characteristics:

- A single block of wood houses all the chanters and drones.
- The instrument has two separate, divergent pipes, on which the performer plays to modulate the sound (double chanter), using one hand for each pipe.
- The air supply is by mouth.
- The reeds, whether for the chanters or the drones, are typically either all single or all double.

Notable examples of southern Italian zampogna bagpipes include:

1. **The *Ciaramelle***, a zampogna originating from Alta Sabina, a region that largely coincides with the province of Rieti (Latium) but also includes some border areas in Umbria and Abruzzo. In this instrument, the smaller drone is absent, while the larger drone pipe is present but inactive. For this reason, the sound is produced solely by the chanters. Research is still ongoing to determine the reasons behind this configuration, but no fully convincing explanation has yet been found (Guizzi, 2020).

   The *ciaramelle* from Amatrice (Rieti) has a different repertoire from other bagpipes in Central and Southern Italy: it is not used during Christmas rituals. Instead, its repertoire is based on pieces that accompany dances such as the *saltarella*, as well as pieces intended purely for listening, called *sonate*, which are performed in sequence during wedding celebrations. Among these, there are pieces such as *la piagnereccia*, played in front of the bride's door and characterized by a mournful tone, evoking sorrow for the girl's departure from her parents' home; *la camminareccia*, which precedes and accompanies the wedding procession; and *la crellareccia*, accompanied by a tambourine's lively rhythm, performed as the newlyweds exit the church.

2. **The *Zampogna Zoppa*** (uneven zampogna) is characteristic of Latium and Molise and is also found in Abruzzo border areas, such as Castellafiume and Capistrello (L'Aquila), as well as the Teramo area. It lacks a key—a metal mechanism used to close the last hole for the low note when it is too distant from the others to be reached by the performer's fingers (Fig. 100). In the past, the *zampogna zoppa* was typically paired with one or more *ciaramelle*—in this case, referring to popular oboe-like aerophones. The *ciaramella*, in the sense of a popular oboe (and therefore lacking a bag), is discussed in section 14.5.1.

Fig. 100 Zampogna zoppa

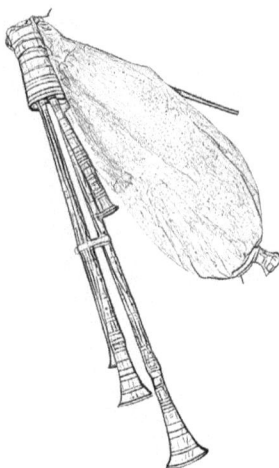

3. **The *Zampogna Numerata*** (numbered zampogna) is a keyed type characteristic of Latium and Molise. It features: 1) a single block of wood housing all the chanters and drones; 2) two unequal, diverging conical chanters; 3) two drones, typically with only the larger one active; 4) double reeds on all the sounding pipes; and 5) a key (a metal device that closes the last hole) on one of the chanters (Fig. 101).

Fig. 101 Zampogna numerata

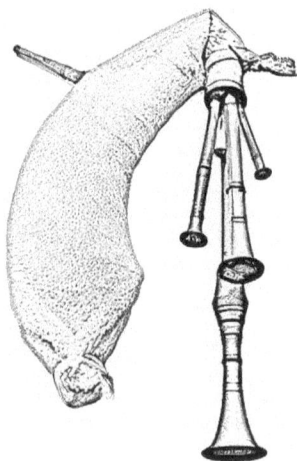

The term "numerata" refers to the existence of various models of this instrument, identified by conventional numbers such as 25 and 28. The *zampogna numerata* is typically used in conjunction with the *ciaramella* or *biffera*, a popular oboe-like aerophone. The latter performs the main melody, while the *zampogna numerata* provides the accompaniment.

4. **The Zampogna from Panni** (Panni is a small village in the province of Foggia) is characterized by a single, relatively short chanter. The drone consists of a sturdy pipe with a small, dried gourd at the end. Both the chanter and the drone are fitted into their respective assembly capsules, and both pipes use single reeds. The bag is made of lambskin, and the pressure on the bag is applied by the performer's arm, whose hand holds the drone (Fig. 102).

Fig. 102 Zampogna from Panni

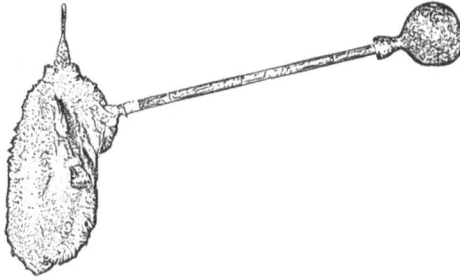

5. **The Large Zampogna from Monreale** (Palermo) is a keyed instrument. As the name suggests, it is a large instrument—often the height of the bagpipe matches or even exceeds that of the performer. Research has reported instances where the left chanter measured nearly two meters (Gioielli, 2015) (Fig. 103).

    This instrument serves two functions, within a religious-devotional context: 1) a solo role during the novena of the Immaculate Conception, the novena of Christmas, and the octave of Epiphany, where *Pasturali* and instrumental litanies are performed; 2) the accompaniment of devotional songs centered on the stories of Jesus' birth and passion, as well as the lives of Mary and the saints.

    It plays in a minor tonality, but it formerly had a second key that allowed for altering the third interval between minor and major.

Fig. 103 Large zampogna from Monreale

6. **The *Zampogna a Paro* or *Ciaramedda***, typical of eastern Sicily and southern Calabria. The name refers to the fact that its two chanters are of equal length. It has two, three, or less frequently, four sounding drones. In most instruments, all the reeds are single (Fig. 104). It is a solo instrument.

Fig. 104 Zampogna a paro

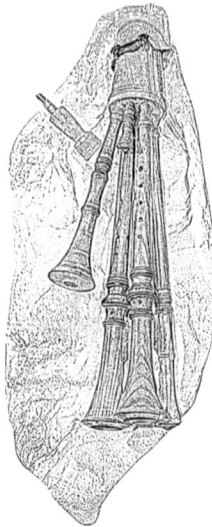

Calabria is a region where the tradition of the zampogna, in its various forms, is strongly felt. Calabrian bagpipes usually have large bags made from the skin of a goat or a sheep, which, once removed from the animal, retain their shape with the fur turned inward. The stock is tied where the animal's neck was, and the blowpipe is attached where one of the front legs was. Most Calabrian bagpipes have two chanters, along with the drones. The reeds can be either single or double. The single reed, called *zommaredda*, is the most commonly used, but some instruments are fitted with both types of reeds simultaneously.

The repertoire of Calabrian bagpipes consists of pieces played throughout the year, primarily during festive ritual occasions. *Pastorali* are played mainly during processions, whereas *tarantelle* are performed during dance events. In both cases, the music is characterized by iterations and microvariations.

In addition to the *zampogna a paro* or *ciaramedda*, other types of Calabrian bagpipes include:

1. **The *Zampogna a Palmi*** (zampogna sized by palms), characteristic of some areas of Calabria, Basilicata, and Campania. It is called "a palmi" because it is made in various sizes, measured using an ancient unit of measurement, the palm, which corresponds to about 26 cm. The left chanter of the *zampogna a palmi* features a key concealed by a key cover. This cover is a wooden shell, perforated to allow the sound to resonate (Fig. 105). The *zampogna a palmi* is traditionally used as an accompanying instrument.

Fig. 105 Zampogna a palmi

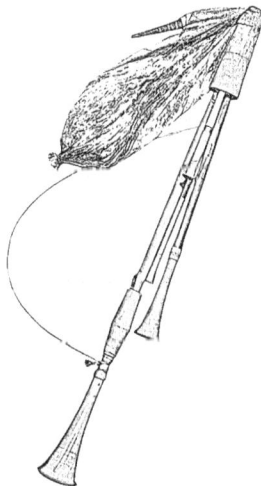

2. **The *Surdulina***, typical of northern Calabria and southern Basilicata. The suffix "-ina" is a diminutive in Italian, suggesting that the *surdulina* is an instrument with very small chanters. According to research, the name *surdulina* derives from the adjective *sorda* (voiceless), implying that when the left chanter is stopped with a wooden or beeswax block and all the holes are closed, it no longer produces any sound (Gala, 1991). It is also called the Albanian zampogna, as it is typical of the Albanian minorities living in these areas. The instrument features two cylindrical chanters of equal length, two or three drones (the longest being the largest pipe of the instrument), and single reeds on both chanters and drones (Fig. 106). Its repertoire includes both solo pieces and pieces featuring tambourine accompaniment, performed in support of songs and dances during folk festivals and religious rites such as the Christmas novena.

Fig. 106 Surdulina

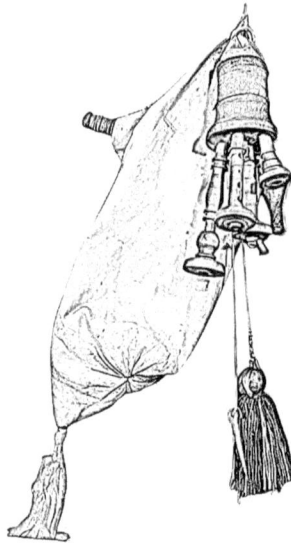

14.4.3.3 History of the Sordellina

Section 14.4.3.2 mentioned the Calabrian bagpipe known as the *surdulina*. This dialectal name seems to correspond to the Italian term *sordellina*. Although both are bagpipes, the two instruments differ in several respects: the most notable difference is that the *surdulina* is inflated through a blowpipe, whereas the *sordellina* was equipped with a bellows.

Research indicates that the *sordellina* was probably invented in Naples in the 15th century (Tarrini, 1995) and featured two keyed chanters and, during the Renaissance, a drone (Degli Esposti, n.d.). It was primarily used by performers from the lower classes and was, therefore, considered a crude and inelegant instrument.

Research has identified around 40 documents from the 15th to the 17th centuries—including literary texts, musical treatises, inventories, and compositions—that attest to the existence of the *sordellina* or *sordina* throughout Italy, produced by bagpipe makers (Tarrini, 1995). Among these documents are the *Dialogues* of the Neapolitan playwright Massimo Troiano, who reported that at the Bavarian court, during the celebrations for the marriage of William VI and Renata of Lorraine, "a man dressed as a peasant [was noticed] […] accompanied by a *sordellina*, who […] made people laugh a lot" (Troiano, 1569: II, 86). A few years later, in 1600, Emilio de' Cavalieri (1550–1602) also mentions this instrument in his *Rappresentatione di anima et di corpo* [Representation of Soul and Body], one of the earliest examples of a drama completely set to music. The score includes an *Aria cantata e sonata al modo antico, da un Flauto ovvero dalle Sordelline* [Aria Sung and Played in the Old Manner, by a Flute or by Sordellinas] (de' Cavalieri, 1600: 50). Also in 1600, Giovanni Lorenzo Baldano from Savona (1576–1660) wrote *Libro per scriver l'intavolatura per sonare sopra le sordelline* [Book for Writing Tablature for Playing on the Sordellinas], which contains about 160 pieces for this instrument, including dances, folk songs, themes with variations, and some chamber music, along with tuning instructions (Baldano, 1600).

The widespread interest in the *sordellina* attests to the great importance attributed to this instrument during this period. Following significant technological advancements, the *sordellina* was capable of performing refined and complex music. Consequently, both the repertoire for the *sordellina* and the instrument itself were no longer regarded as simple and popular but rather as noble and sophisticated.

By the 17th century, the *sordellina* had evolved into a "courtly" bagpipe, highly appreciated by musicians, aristocrats, and wealthy merchants. It had a rich repertoire for the accompaniment of both religious and secular songs, as well as dances, which were performed with great success at the European courts of the time. Research has shown that, during the 17th century, *sordellina* models were built with many keys: 25, 42, and even 56 (Gioielli, 2015). Scholars of the time claimed that no *sordellina* was more perfect than the one with 56 keys (Terzago, 1664).

Among those who contributed to the dissemination of the *sordellina* were François Langlois, Manfredo Settala, and Marin Mersenne.

François Langlois (1588–1647) was a French painter, engraver, and art dealer well-known throughout Europe, which he traveled extensively for professional reasons. He was an expert performer on the *musette de cour*, an instrument that, according to a scholar, dates to the 13th century but was only equipped with a bellows around 1600 (McLeod, 1999). Additionally, Langlois was an acclaimed performer of the *sordellina*, which he presented and demonstrated during his travels between 1623 and 1626 in Rome, Paris, Bordeaux, and London, thus spreading knowledge of this aerophone.

The Milanese Manfredo Settala (1600–1680) was an ingenious inventor and maker of musical instruments, often referred to as the "father of the Italian *sordellina*." He designed and created various models of *sordelline*, the most complex of which was a four-pipe instrument with 56 keys. A 1640 portrait by the painter Carlo Francesco Nuvolone depicts Settala showcasing various inventions and creations, including a *sordellina*.

In his treatise *Harmonie universelle*, published between 1636 and 1637, French scholar Marin Mersenne (1588–1648) dedicates the fifth book to wind instruments. He describes with great accuracy a *sordellina* made by Manfredo Settala and recommends that the French musette also be equipped with "four parts [pipes], to play all kinds of music" and "songs in four parts," just as the *sordellina* could do (Mersenne, 1963 [1636]: III, 292–293). Given the widespread influence of Mersenne's work, it is likely that the Italian *sordellina* had a significant impact on various European bagpipes.

14.4.3.4 Single-Reed and Double-Reed Bagpipes

Another key distinction, beyond that between northern Italian pivas and southern Italian zampognas, is between single-reed instruments, like clarinets, and double-reed instruments, like oboes.

In the first group are bagpipes with cylindrical bores and single reeds. Research suggests a likely Greek-Balkan origin for these instruments, connected to migrations from those regions during Greek colonization, Byzantine rule, and later during the Ottoman expansion (Guizzi, 2020). Examples of these bagpipes include the Istrian piva, the *zampogna a paro*, and the *surdulina*.

In the second group are bagpipes with conical bores and double reeds. For this type of bagpipe, research suggests a probable derivation from the Roman *tibiae* (Guizzi, 2020). Examples include the *zampogna zoppa*, the *zampogna a chiave* (zampogna with key), and the large zampogna from Monreale.

14.4.3.5 Zampogna Bagpipes in Abruzzese Iconography

The zampogna is frequently depicted in Abruzzese iconography as early as the 14th century, appearing in frescoes, bas-reliefs, and statues. While there is always some uncertainty regarding the accuracy of these images in representing historical reality, the painting *Nativity* by Andrea De Litio, part of the pictorial cycle in the choir of the canons in the Cathedral of Atri (Teramo), offers points of great interest. It depicts various scenes of pastoral and rural life, centered on shepherds and flocks, including a dance scene featuring a bagpiper. The zampogna shown has a single chanter, played by the performer with both hands, and a drone. The performer holds the bag in front of him and compresses it with his left elbow (Fig. 107).

Fig. 107 Andrea de Litio, *Nativity*, detail

The miniature dedicated to the Nativity, contained in the *Missale Plenum* (Complete Missal) from the second half of the 14th century, originally held by the Church of San Francesco in Guardiagrele (Chieti) and now kept in the Cathedral of Chieti, depicts a bagpiper holding a small bagpipe with both arms. The instrument is characterized by equal-sized chanters joined in a single block (Fig. 108).

Fig. 108 *Missale Plenum*, miniature, detail

In the Cathedral of Teramo, there is a silver *paliotto* by Nicola da Guardiagrele. The *paliotto* is the covering that adorns the front of the altar. In the second panel of this *paliotto*, which focuses on the Nativity, a bagpiper is depicted playing a small bagpipe with a single chanter.

In Caramanico (Pescara), on one of the side walls of the 15th-century Church of Santa Maria delle Grazie, stands a stone statue of a bagpiper holding a small bagpipe. The two chanters are joined in a single block, showing several similarities to the zampogna depicted in the *Missale Plenum* from Guardiagrele.

Lastly, there is a polychrome wooden sculpture from the 15th century, originating from the parish church of Atessa (Chieti), depicting a bagpiper. The instrument has two equal-sized chanters, and the performer compresses the bag with his right elbow (Fig. 109).

Fig. 109 Polychrome wooden statue

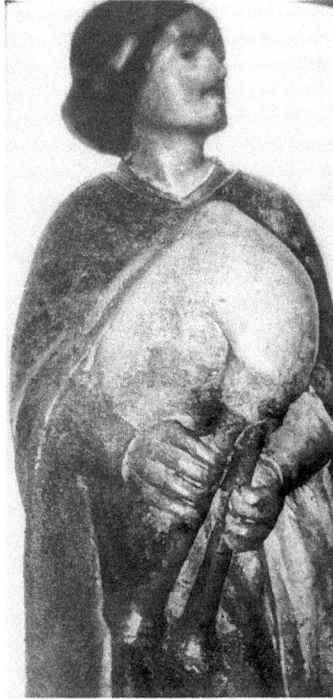

14.4.3.6 Zampogna in 20th-Century Poetic Works

Zampogna bagpipers and bagpipes have been the subject of many poems. Among the most famous poets is Giovanni Pascoli, who, while in Messina in December 1901, wrote his poem *Le ciaramelle*, later included in his collection *Canti di Castelvecchio* [Songs of Castelvecchio]. The term *ciaramelle* is the Italianized form of the Sicilian dialect term *ciaramedde*, which refers to zampogna bagpipes. Also in 1901, the playwright and poet Luigi Pirandello paid poetic tribute to the zampogna by writing an entire collection of poems titled *Zampogna*.

Other poets who have dedicated verses to zampogna bagpipes and bagpipers include Gianni Rodari, with the poem *Lo zampognaro*; Virginio Di Carmine, with *Alle ciaramelle, Zampogne e zampognari amatriciani*, and *Suono di ciaramelle*; Federico Tosti, with *Notte ar Gran Sasso*; and Tommaso Tozzi, with the poem *Zampogne*.

14.5 Reedpipes

Among aerophones, one sub-class consists of wind instruments proper, in which the vibrating air is contained within the instrument itself. A category of wind instruments proper consists of reedpipes, which have attached reeds. These reeds are oscillating lamellae that regulate airflow, intermittently allowing it to enter and vibrate the air column inside the instrument.

14.5.1 Ciaramella

Section 14.4.3.2 mentioned the term *ciaramelle*, which designates a specific type of zampogna. However, in its singular form, *ciaramella* can also refer to an aerophone in the oboe family. The term *ciaramella* might derive from the Late Latin *calamellus*, a diminutive of the Latin *calamus*, meaning cane. If this hypothesis is accepted, it would be logical to understand *ciaramella* as designating a reedpipe. Other names for this instrument include *bbifara*, *bifara*, *cornetta*, *pipita*, *totarella*, and *trombetta*.

Popular oboes found in the central-southern regions of Abruzzo, Latium, Molise, Campania, Basilicata, and Calabria share several common features: a conical tube, a flared bell, a long double reed, and the absence of a pirouette (a device where the performer rests their lips). The two main models of *ciaramella* are the *lucana* (from Basilicata), with seven front holes and one rear hole, and the *molisana* (from Molise), with eight front holes and one rear hole (Fig. 110). Due to the different numbers of holes in the two models, switching between them requires the performer to adapt their playing technique.

The range of both types is slightly more than an octave, but the *ciaramella lucana* is characterized by a softer timbre and a more moderate tone, while the *ciaramella molisana* has a clearer timbre and a brighter voice.

In researching the origins of the *ciaramella*, a scholar has found that, toward the end of the 1st century CE, a similar instrument to the oboe, featuring a conical tube and a double reed, was known in Rome (Guizzi, 2020). However, its earliest origins are likely linked to the Middle Eastern region (Karstädt, 1984). The Middle Eastern origin of the instrument might also explain another possible etymology of the term *ciaramella*: according to a scholar, the name could also derive from the Arabic *salamiyyah*, a designation for a reed aerophone widespread in Egypt, traditionally used to accompany songs, storytelling, and poetry recitation (Hanna, 2007).

Fig. 110 Ciaramella lucana and ciaramella molisana

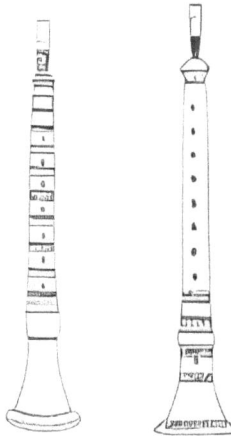

During the Crusades, an ancient type of *ciaramella* was used by Muslims in battle as a psychological weapon, terrifying the Crusaders with its penetrating sound. Recognizing its utility as a far-reaching sound source the Crusaders brought it to Europe. There, it was initially used in a military context to transmit signals for cavalry maneuvers and later to announce public events. Starting in the 14th century, following technical developments that softened its sound, the instrument became suitable for purely musical contexts. It was included as *discantus* in instrumental groups performing *musica alta*—loud outdoor music—alongside shawms, slide trumpets, and timpani, participating in musical performances at aristocratic events such as weddings and court festivities, as well as in popular contexts like fairs and dances.

In contemporary traditional music, the *ciaramella* is typically paired with the zampogna in multi-voiced performances. While this type of ensemble is mainly heard during the Christmas season, when performers dressed as shepherds travel through towns and cities, the instrumental pairing originally had broader use and could also accompany *tarantelle* and other dances.

14.5.2 Launeddas

The launeddas (also called *leuneddas* or *liuneddas*) belong to the class of aerophones, within the sub-class of wind instruments proper. They are included in the category of reedpipes and, within this category, they belong to the group called "sets of reedpipes with single reeds". Thus, they are a wind instrument with single reeds, occupying a unique place in the traditional music of Sardinia. The origins of this instrument are very ancient, and research has identified many similarities between the Sardinian launeddas and other aerophones, such as ancient Egyptian clarinets, Greek auloi, and Roman *tibiae* (Paulis, 1994).

Over time, scholars have proposed various hypotheses regarding the etymology of the term "launeddas". Glottologist Salvatore Dedola notes that Matteo Madau and Giovanni Spano, in the 18th and 19th centuries respectively, linked the term to *leone* (lion), suggesting that the pipes may have originally been made from the bones of this animal. By the end of the 19th century, Tito Zanardelli argued that launeddas could derive from the Latin *calamus*. In the early 20th century, Giulio Fara and Pier Enea Guarnerio proposed that it might derive from *lionaxi* (oleander). In 1963, Francesco Alziator hypothesized that launeddas could come from *lacunedda* (stream), as the material used for the instrument grows in water-rich areas (cited in Dedola, 2017). Giulio Paulis suggested that the term might derive from the Latin *ligulella* (a diminutive of *ligula*), meaning "small tongue," referring to an instrument with reeds (Paulis, 1994). Max Leopold Wagner suggested that the origin could be traced to the Greek *monaulos* (wind instrument having a single tube) (Wagner, 2008), while Alberto Areddu supports the hypothesis that the word evolved from the Greek *ligyn* (shrill tone) passing through Etruscan and Faliscan, to the Latin *ligunella*, and finally to the Sardinian word launeddas (Areddu, 2010).

14.5.2.1 The Construction of the Launeddas

The instrument essentially consists of three pipes of different lengths, diameters, and thicknesses. Two of these pipes, the *tumbu* and the *mancosa manna*, are bound together with a piece of tarred thread, while the third pipe, the *mancosedda*, remains separate. The two bound pipes, which together form *sa loba*, have an upper and a lower binding. The lower binding includes a small spacer that ensures the two pipes form an angle of about 10°.

At the upper end of each pipe, a thinner pipe called *cabitzinu* is inserted, which the performer fully places in their mouth. The *cabitzinu* is used to create the reed, known as *linguatza*, by cutting three sides of the pipe's surface. This allows the upper part of the reed to remain fixed while the lower part can vibrate when activated by the performer's breath (Fig. 111). Scholar Giulio Fara noted that the instrument's configuration and the arrangement of the reeds resemble those of the *auloi gamelioi*, an ancient Greek instrument consisting of two similarly shaped but differently sized pipes, each equipped with a single reed (Fara, 1997). Botanist Theophrastus, who lived between the 4th and the 3rd centuries BCE, provided a detailed description of this instrument (Theophrastus, n.d.).

Fig. 111 Launeddas

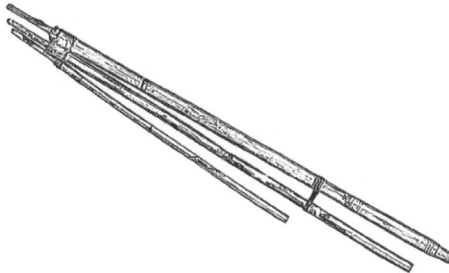

The tuning of the launeddas is achieved by adjusting the weight of the reeds, applying more or less beeswax to the free end of the reeds.

The *tumbu* pipe, which is thin-walled and slightly conical, can reach about 150 cm in length and is typically made of two or more rarely three segments joined together. Thanks to this segmented structure, it can be stored in its case, called *straccasciu*, and easily transported. The *tumbu* has no finger holes and therefore always produces the same tone, serving as the tonic of the instrument and functioning as the drone. It is held with the left hand.

The *mancosa manna*, which is bound to the *tumbu* to form *sa loba*, consists of a single cane segment with four rectangular finger holes on the front wall, called *crais*, and a fifth, elongated hole lower down, called *s'arrefinu* or *bentiadori*, used for tuning the instrument. It produces the accompaniment notes and is played by the performer with the left hand.

The *mancosedda*, which is not attached to the other two pipes, produces the melody notes and is played with the right hand.

Various types of cane are used in the construction of the instrument. For the *tumbu*, a straight, thin-walled cane of the variety *Arundo donax* is used, while for the *mancosa manna* and the *mancosedda*, a thicker cane with a smaller internal cavity is required. This necessitates the use of a different variety of cane, *Arundo plinii*, known as *cann'e Seddori*, which grows only in the Marmilla and

Trexenta regions of central-southern Sardinia. The greater thickness of this cane contributes to the distinctive timbre of the launeddas.

It is important to note that the sound characteristics of the launeddas depend on several factors: the key is determined by the size of the pipes, while the range and intervallic relationships between their sounds depend on the position of the holes. The harmonic relationships between the pipes are influenced by the criteria used in their selection and combination.

14.5.2.2 The Historical Context of the Launeddas

According to Andreas Bentzon, the launeddas are a direct descendant of the ancient double clarinets used by the Egyptians and the Sumerians, retaining certain structural and performance similarities to those instruments (Bentzon, 2002).

In fact, the earliest evidence of the use of launeddas dates back to prehistory: a bronze statuette found in Ittiri (Sassari), originating from the Nuragic civilization, which emerged in Sardinia during the Bronze Age, has been dated by scholars to the 8th century BCE and likely depicts a launeddas player (Santoni, 1997) (Fig. 112).

Fig. 112 Bronze statuette

The depiction of the performer is not highly detailed, but the sculptor paid significant attention to reproducing the musical instrument and how it is handled. The instrument has three pipes: two are paired and joined together, held in the musician with their left hand, while the third pipe is held by the performer's right hand and angled outward, diverging slightly from the first two. Despite the small size of the statuette, which measures only 80 mm, research has noted that the artist carved a longitudinal groove into the small tube representing the two parallel pipes, allowing them to be identified as two distinct but adjacent tubes (Fara, 1997).

Giulio Fara also emphasized that the arrangement of the pipes and the playing technique have remained consistent from prehistoric times to the present-day launeddas. This suggests that the materials used for constructing the various parts of the instrument and the technique for making the reed have also remained unchanged (Fara, 1997).

14.5.2.3 Usage Occasions

One of the occasions for using the launeddas was the *ballu tundu*, a dance commonly performed until around the mid-20th century. Dancers would form a circle, hold hands, and slowly move around the launeddas player positioned at the center, performing steps that often differed for men and women and varied depending on the sections of each piece.

Public dances were held on Sundays in the square in front of the church, with some pieces, danced only by men, performed starting on Saturday afternoon. The following day, a brief dance took place after Mass, followed by more dances in the afternoon and evening. These events offered young people the opportunity to meet and interact, although strict rules governed the distance between males and females unless they were married or engaged to each other. Other occasions for dance accompaniment included festivals honoring the patron saint and wedding celebrations (Sedda, 2003).

The musical phrases accompanying the dances were often of considerable technical difficulty and were closely guarded by performers. For reasons of personal prestige and to maintain professional opportunities, top players were reluctant to share their trade secrets with other performers or even with young apprentices (Bentzon, 2002).

The launeddas were also used to accompany songs, though competition among performers in this context was much less intense. The repertoire for song accompaniment was considered less important within the professional scope of a launeddas player. A typical performance involved several stages: tuning the pipes, an instrumental introduction, accompaniment phrases to which the singer's voice was added, and instrumental interludes during breaks in the singing. Bentzon notes that in songs accompanied by the launeddas, a particular singing style was used, characterized by a guttural tone and almost devoid of ornamentation. He hypothesizes that singers unconsciously imitated the timbre of the launeddas with their voices (Bentzon, 2002).

Finally, in the past, the launeddas played an important role in both religious and civic contexts. For this reason, a player's repertoire often included hymns and marches for various festive occasions. In religious settings, the launeddas were used during the Mass and religious processions, suggesting that the use of the instrument in such ceremonies was either approved or at least tolerated by the Church. Additionally, it was traditional for the launeddas to accompany the collection of alms for organizing the patron saint's festival and to be played during wedding parades (Bentzon, 2002).

14.5.2.4 Relevance of the Launeddas

To this day, the launeddas remain significant in community life, both at major public and private events, and attract large audiences during launeddas performance competitions. From the performer's perspective, this importance not only ensures social prestige but also good earnings. The ongoing use of the launeddas suggests that their practice today is not merely the result of revival efforts.

Interest in the launeddas has inspired the Conservatorio of Cagliari to include courses on this instrument in its educational offerings, beginning with preparatory courses in 2017, and, from 2018, as a specific focus within the bachelor's degree program in traditional music.

Summary

The aerophone class comprises several groups of instruments, including: 1) free aerophones, 2) free reed aerophones, 3) straight flutes, 4) bagpipes, and 5) reedpipes. An example of a free aerophone is the bullroarer. Among the free reed aerophones is the diatonic accordion, an instrument that shares intriguing similarities and differences with to the bandoneon. The straight flutes group includes the Calabrian *fischiottu*, the Sicilian *friscalettu*, various Sardinian recorders, and the Abruzzese *chioffërë*.

The analysis of bagpipes focuses on various types of zampogna from central-southern Italy, highlighting their similarities and differences with other bagpipes, known as pivas, common in northern Italy. The chapter also includes written and iconographic evidence tracing the history and evolution of these instruments over the centuries. Among reedpipes, the *ciaramella* and the launeddas are examined, with a discussion of the repertoire and contexts of use for each instrument.

Keywords

Aerophones, *Anche Libre*, Bag Aerophones, *Baga, Baghet, Ballu Tundu,* Bandoneon, Bass Casing, Bellows, Bisonoric, Bullroarer, *Burriburri, Cabitzinu, Cann'e Seddori, Chioffërë, Ciaramedda, Ciaramella, Ciaramelle,* Collection of Alms, *Ddu Botte,* Diatonic Accordion, *Diatonisch Nieuwsblad, Fiscaruolu, Fischiottu,* Free Aerophones, Free Reed Aerophones, *Friscalettu, Frusciu, Gaita de botão,* Hand Strap, Kusserow System, *Lapuni,* Launeddas, *Linguatza, Mancosa Manna, Mancosedda, Musa/müsa,* Musette, *Phagotus, Pipaiolu, Pipiolu,* Piva, Plate, Recorder Flutes, Reed, *Sa Loba, Salamiyyah, Sheng, Sordellina, Sulittu, Sulittu and Tamburinu Surdulina,* Treble Casing, *Tumbu,* Zampogna, *Zampogna a Paro, Zampogna Numerata, Zampogna Zoppa.*

Preeminent Figures

- Afranio degli Albonesi
- Alberto Areddu
- Andreas Bentzon
- Aristophanes
- Arnold van Westerhout
- Athanasius Kircher
- Cyril Demian
- Dio Chrysostom
- Filippo Bonanni

- Francesco Alziator
- Francesco Bianchini
- François Langlois
- Giovanni Lorenzo Baldano
- Giovanni Spano
- Giulio Fara
- Giulio Paulis
- Hans Geller
- Hector Berlioz
- Johann Wilde
- Manfredo Settala
- Marin Mersenne
- Martial
- Massimo Troiano
- Matteo Madau
- Max Leopold Wagner
- Michael Praetorius
- Nero
- Orazio Maccari
- Pier Enea Guarnerio
- Rabanus Maurus
- Suetonius

Questions for Review

1. From an organological perspective, how is the bullroarer classified?
2. What is a reed?
3. From an organological perspective, how is the diatonic accordion classified?
4. What is the structure of the diatonic accordion?
5. What does "bisonoric diatonic accordion" mean?
6. What do the terms two-voice, three-voice, and four-voice diatonic accordions refer to?
7. On what basis are different types of diatonic accordions distinguished?
8. What does the term *ddu botte* refer to?
9. What is the range of the *ddu botte*?
10. What is the *sheng*?

11. What does the term "semi-chromatic accordion" refer to?
12. In which Italian regions is the diatonic accordion popular, and what is its repertoire in those regions?
13. Is the diatonic accordion popular outside of Italy?
14. What is the traditional repertoire of the diatonic accordion?
15. Is there a difference between traditional practice and revival practice for the diatonic accordion?
16. What are the similarities and differences between the diatonic accordion and the bandoneon?
17. How can recorders generally be described?
18. What are the main types of Calabrian *fischiotti*?
19. What are the typical occasions and repertoire for the *friscalettu*?
20. Can *friscalettu* instruments be decorated?
21. What are the main types of recorders from Sardinia?
22. What do the terms *sulittu* and *tamburinu* refer to?
23. What is the *chioffërë*?
24. How are bagpipes classified?
25. What evidence do we have of bagpipes from the 1st century CE onward?
26. Which Italian poets and writers from the 14th to the 17th centuries mention bagpipes?
27. When was the *phagotus* invented?
28. Which early ethno-organologists mention bagpipes starting from the 17th century onwards?
29. What are the main characteristics of northern Italian bagpipes?
30. In which regions are northern Italian bagpipes popular?
31. What is the likely etymology of the term zampogna?
32. What are the main characteristics of southern Italian bagpipes?
33. In which regions are southern Italian bagpipes popular?
34. What types of bagpipes are popular in Calabria?
35. When was the *sordellina* invented?
36. Was the *sordellina* a rustic or courtly instrument?
37. Who contributed to the spread of the *sordellina*?
38. What is meant by the terms "single-reed bagpipes" and "double-reed bagpipes"?
39. Are there various depictions of the zampogna in Abruzzese iconography?
40. Are there 20th-century poetic works dedicated to the zampogna?
41. What are reedpipes?

42. What is the *ciaramella*?

43. For what characteristics was the *ciaramella* initially used in a military context?

44. What instruments were part of *musica alta* ensembles?

45. From an organological perspective, how is the instrument known as launeddas classified?

46. What hypotheses have been proposed regarding the etymology of the term launeddas?

47. What is the structure of the launeddas?

48. What materials are used to make the launeddas?

49. What information can be deduced from the bronze statuette found in Ittiri?

50. On what occasions were/are the launeddas most frequently used, and what repertoire is performed on this instrument?

Further Reading and Online Resources

Albonesi, Teseo Ambrogio. *Introductio in Chaldaicam linguam, Syriacam atque Armenicam et decem alias linguas characterum differentium Alphabeta, circiter quadraginta, et eorundem invicem conformatio. Mystica et cabalistica quamplurima scitu digna. Et descriptio ac simulachrum Phagoti Afranij, Theseo Ambrosio ex Comitibus Albonesii I. V. Doct. Papien. Canonico Regulari Lateranensi, ac Sancti Petri in Coelo Aureo Papiae Praepositio, Authore,* MDXXXIX, A f. 213 v. Excudebat Papiae Ioan. Maria Simoneta Cremonensis. In Canonica Sancti Petri in Caelo Aureo, Sumptibus & Typis, Authoris libri, 1539.

Areddu, Alberto. "Il nome delle 'launeddas': un'ipotesi etrusco-italica." *Insula*, 7, 2010: 5–35.

Aristophanes. *The Comedies of Aristophanes, a New and Literal Translation from the Revised Text of Dindorf with Notes and Extracts from the Best Metrical Versions*. Translated by William James Hicke. London: George Bell & Sons, 1901.

Baines, Anthony. *Bagpipes*. Oxford: Pitt Rivers Museum, 1960.

Baldano, Giovanni Lorenzo. *Libro per scriver l'intavolatura per sonare sopra le sordelline*, ms. 1600.

Bentzon, Andreas Fridolin Weis. *Launeddas*, 2 vols. Cagliari, Italy: Iscandula, 2002.

Berlioz, Hector. *Voyage musical en Allemagne et en Italie. Etudes sur Beethoven, Gluck et Weber. Mélanges et Nouvelles*, 2 vols. Paris: Jules Labitte, 1844.

Bianchini, Francesco. *De tribus generibus instrumentorum musicae veterum organicae dissertatio*. Roma: Bernabó & Lazzarini (Fausto Amadei), 1742.

Bonanni, Filippo. *Gabinetto armonico pieno d'istromenti sonori, indicati e spiegati dal padre Filippo Bonanni della Compagnia di Gesù offerto al Santo Re David*. Roma: Giorgio Placho, 1722.

Calà, Gemino. *Lo zufolo. U friscalettu. Metodo musicale*. Brolo, Italy: Armenio, 2001.

Chrysostom, Dio. *Discourses 61–80. Fragments. Letters*. Translated by H. Lamar Crosby. Loeb Classical Library 385. Cambridge, MA: Harvard University Press, 1951.

de' Cavalieri, Emilio. *Rappresentatione di Anima, et di Corpo. Nuovamente posta in Musica dal Sig. Emilio del Caualliere, per recitar Cantando. Data in luce da Alessandro Guidotti Bolognese*. Roma: Nicolò Mutij, 1600.

Dedola, Salvatore. "Launeddas." October 10, 2017. Accessed November 3, 2024. https://www.sunuraghe.it/2017/ottobre-una-parola-sarda-al-mese-l-come-laune%E1%B8%91%E1%B8%91as.

Degli Esposti, Goffredo. "La Sordellina." n.d. Accessed November 3, 2024. https://www.goffredodegliesposti.it/sordellina-3/.

Di Silvestre, Carlo. *Strumenti musicali di tradizione popolare*. Pineto, Italy: Il Passagallo, 2004.

Dlačić, Marijana, and Hrvoje Badurina. *Tajna melodija ovčje kože*. Lubenice, Croatia: Centar za održivi razvoj "Gerbin," 2012.

Fara, Giulio. *L'anima della Sardegna*. Udine, Italy: Istituto delle edizioni accademiche, 1940.

Fara, Giulio. *Sulla musica popolare in Sardegna*, edited by Gian Nicola Spanu. Nuoro, Italy: Ilisso, 1997.

Gala, Giuseppe Michele. *La zampogna lucana*, with an attached CD. Firenze, Italy: Taranta, 1991.

Gala, Giuseppe Michele. *Le tradizioni musicali in Lucania*. Firenze, Italy: Taranta, 2007.

Gatto, Danilo. *Suonare la tradizione: Manuale di musica popolare calabrese.* Soveria Mannelli, Italy: Rubbettino Editore, 2007.

Geller, Hans. *Die Bildnisse der deutschen Künstler in Rom, 1800–1830.* Berlin: Deutscher Verein für Kunstwissenschaft, 1952.

Gellerman, Robert F. *The American Reed Organ and the Harmonium: A Treatise on Its History, Restoration and Tuning, with Descriptions of Some Outstanding Collections, Including a Stop Dictionary and a Directory of Reed Organs.* Vestal, NY: Vestal Press, 1996.

Giannattasio, Francesco. "L'organetto nella musica popolare sarda." In *Strumenti della musica popolare sarda*, edited by Gian Nicola Spanu, 100–105. Nuoro, Italy: ISRE Ilisso, 1994.

Gioielli, Mauro. "Curiosità zampognare." *Utriculus*, 16 (October–December), 1995: 11–12.

Gioielli, Mauro. "La zampogna: storia di uno strumento musicale." *Utriculus*, 32 (October–December), 1999: 10–31.

Gioielli, Mauro. "Gli aerofoni a sacco italiani dall'antichità all'epoca moderna." *Utriculus*, 49–50, 2015: 29–42.

Guizzi, Fabio. *Guida alla musica popolare in Italia.* Lucca, Italy: LIM, 2020.

Hanna, Hany Aziz, "Traditional Egyptian Storytellers Heritage and Its Instruments and Tools." 2007. Accessed November 3, 2024. https://cool.culturalheritage.org/byform/mailing-lists/cdl/2007/0708.html.

Karstädt, Georg. "Oboe." In *Dizionario enciclopedico universale della musica e dei musicisti*, edited by Alberto Basso, Torino, Italy: UTET, 1984.

Maccari, Orazio. "Sopra un'antica statuetta di marmo rappresentante un suonator di cornamusa del museo del Sig. Marchese D. Marcello Venuti." In *Saggi di dissertazioni accademiche pubblicamente lette nella Nobile Accademia Etrusca dell'antichissima Città di Cortona*, VII, 99–108. Roma: Stamperia di Pallade, 1758.

Mahillon, Victor-Charles. *Catalogue descriptif et analytique du Musée instrumental du Conservatoire royal de musique de Bruxelles.* Ghent, Belgium: Hoste, 1880–1892.

Martial, "Epigrams." 2008. Accessed November 3, 2024. https://topostext.org/work/677.

Maurus, Rabanus. "De universo." n.d. Accessed November 3, 2024. https://la.wikisource.org/wiki/De_universo_(Rabanus_Maurus).

McLeod, Ken. "From Hotteterre to the Union Pipes." *The Seán Reid Society Journal*, 1(March), 1999: 1–6.

Mersenne, Marin. *Harmonicorum instrumentorum libri IV*. Lutetiae Parisiorum: (Paris) Gvillielmi Bavdry, 1636.

Mersenne, Marin. *Harmonie Universelle: Contenant la théorie et la pratique de la musique* (Paris, 1636). *Edition fac-similé de l'exemplaire conservé à la Bibliothèque des* Arts *et Métiers et annoté par l'auteur,* Introduction par François Lesure, 3 vols. Paris: CNRS Centre National de la Recherche Scientifique, 1963.

Nastasi, Francesco, and Andrea Capezzuoli. ... *Per fare legria ai siuri de Milan: musica delle Quattro Province per piffero e müsa*, with attached CD. Casale Monferrato, Italy: Folkclub Ethnosuoni, 2010.

Paulis, Giulio. "I nomi delle launeddas: origine e storia." In *SONOS: Strumenti della musica popolare sarda*, edited by Gian Nicola Spanu, 137–139. Nuoro, Italy: ISRE Ilisso Edizioni, 1994.

Praetorius, Michael. *Syntagma musicum*, II: *De organographia*. Wolfenbüttel, Germany: Elias Holwein, 1619.

Sachs, Curt. *Real-Lexikon der Musikinstrumente, zugleich ein Polyglossar für das gesamte Instrumentengebiet*. Berlin: Julius Bard, 1913.

Sachs, Curt. *The History of Musical Instruments*. New York: W.W. Norton, 1940.

Salton, Ricardo D. "El bandoneón." *Revista del Instituto de Investigación Musicológica "Carlos Vega"*, 4, 1981.

Sannino, Maria. "The Zampogna." 2017. Accessed November 3, 2024. https://mariasannino.com/2017/12/11/the-zampogna/.

Santoni, Vincenzo. "La rappresentazione scenica del bronzetto di Ittiri e la produzione figurata barbaricino-mediterraneizzante." In *Launeddas. L'anima di un popolo*, edited by Giampaolo Lallai, 210–219. Cagliari, Italy: AM&D; Nuoro, Italy: ISRE, 1997.

Sarica, Mario. *Strumenti musicali popolari in Sicilia: provincia di Messina*. Messina, Italy: Assessorato alla Cultura—Provincia Regionale di Messina, 2004.

Schaeffner, André. *Origine des instruments de musique. Introduction ethnologique à l'histoire de la musique instrumentale.* Paris: Payot, 1936.

Sedda Franciscu. *Tradurre la tradizione. Sardegna: su ballu, i corpi, la cultura.* Roma: Meltemi, 2003.

Spanu, Gian Nicola. "Strumenti e musiche con strumenti." *Il folklore d'Italia,* 3, 2008: 55–65.

Staiti, Nico. *Angeli e pastori. L'immagine musicale della Natività e le musiche pastorali natalizie.* Bologna, Italy: Ut Orpheus, 1997.

Suetonius. *De Vita Caesarum Libri VIII.* Charleston, SC: Nabu Press, 2011.

Tarrini, Maurizio, ed. "Documenti e testimonianze sulla sordellina (secc. XV-XVII)." In Giovanni Lorenzo Baldano, *Libro per scriver l'intavolatura per sonare sopra le sordelline, Savona 1600,* 107–146. Savona, Italy: Editrice Liguria, 1995.

Terzago, Paolo Maria. *Mvsaeum Septalianvm Manfredi Septalae patritii Mediolanensis indvstrioso Labore constructum; Pavli Mariae Terzagi Mediolanensis physici collegiati geniali laconismo descriptvm (...),* Dertonae (Tortona, Italy): Typis Filiorum quondam Elisei Violae, 1664.

Theophrastus. "Historia plantarum." IV, n.d. Accessed November 3, 2024. http://www.poesialatina.it/_ns/Greek/testi/Theophrastus/Historia_plantarum04.html.

Tombesi, Roberto, and Riccardo Tesi. *L'organetto diatonico: storia, struttura, tecnica e didattica.* Ancona, Italy: Bèrben, 1993.

Troiano, Massimo. *Dialoghi di Massimo Troiano, ne' quali si narrano le cose più notabili fatte nelle Nozze dello Illustriss. & Eccell. Prencipe GUGLIELMO VI, Conte Palatino del Reno, e Duca di Baviera; e dell'Illustriss. & Eccell. Madama RENATA di Loreno.* Venezia, Italy: Bolognino Zaltieri, 1569.

von Hornbostel, Erich Maria, and Curt Sachs. "Systematik der Musikinstrumente. Ein Versuch." *Zeitschrift für Ethnologie,* 4–5, 1914: 553–590.

Wagner, Max Leopold. *DES Dizionario Etimologico Sardo,* edited by Giulio Paulis. Nuoro, Italy: Ilisso Edizioni, 2008.

CHAPTER 15

Table of Instruments

This table categorizes the mentioned instruments as idiophones, membrano-phones, chordophones, or aerophones, offering a quick overview of the primary characteristic that determines the class to which each instrument belongs.

Idiophones	Membranophones	Chordophones	Aerophones
Bell	Battefoche	Colascione	Accordion
Campanedda	Bbù-bbù	Galischan	Alboka
Campaneddu	Bufù	Galischona	Arganettu
Campani	Caccavella	Galizona	Auloi gamelioi
Cowbell	Ciciombre	Gallichone	Aulos
Crillone	Cupa cupa	Saz	Baga
Cymbals	Cuticù	Tanbur	Baghet
Jaw harp	Firri firri		Bandoneon
Mariolu	Putipù		Bbifara
Marranzanu	Tabbala		Bifara
Mascrille	Tamburellu		Biffera
Matracca	Tamburu		Brogna
Matràccola	Tammureddu Tammurinu		Buccina
Mattiaminde	Tamorra/tammorra		Bullroarer
Muligna	Trìmpanu		Burriburri
Mulignedda	Tumbarineddu		Chioffërë
Nganna-larruni	Tumbarinu		Chorus

(Continued)

Idiophones	Membranophones	Chordophones	Aerophones
Rana 'e canna	Vurre vurre		Ciaramedda
Rana 'e taula	Vurrecone		Ciaramella
Scetavajasse	Zuco zuco		Ciaramelle
Sistrum	Zumbu zumbu		Conch shell trumpet
Small bell			Cornetta
Sonazzos			Corru marinu
Spadaccine			Ddu botte
Stròcculas			Diatonic accordion
Taulittas			Diaulos
Tippe-tappe			Farautu
Tràccola			Fiscaruolu
Trènula			Fischiottu
Triangulu			Frautu
Triccheballacche			Friscalettu
Trionfe			Frusciu
Troccola			Gaita de botão
Tròccula			Lapuni
Tromma de li zingari			Launeddas
Trozzula			Leuneddas
Trumbon			Liuneddas
Trunfa			Musa/müsa
Valichira			Musetta/musette
Zaccarredda			Ogganettu
			Organette
			Organettu
			Organittu
			Phagotus
			Phrygian oboe
			Pìffaru
			Piffero
			Pipaiolu

Idiophones	Membranophones	Chordophones	Aerophones
			Pipiolu
			Pipita
			Piva
			Roman tibiae
			Salamiyyah
			Sheng
			Sonettu
			Sordellina
			Sulittu
			Sulittu and tamburinu
			Surdulina
			Tibiae serranae
			Totarella
			Trombetta
			Trumma
			Utriculus
			Zampogna

INDEX OF INSTRUMENTS

INDEX OF NAMES

INDEX OF FIGURES